The Intellectual Legacy
of Paul Tillich

Paul Tillich

The Intellectual Legacy of Paul Tillich

James R. Lyons, Editor

Wayne State University

SLAUGHTER FOUNDATION LECTURES—1966

Wayne State University Press, Detroit, 1969

230.04
T465Ye

175077

*Grateful acknowledgment is made to the William E. Slaughter,
Jr. Foundation for financial assistance in publishing this volume.*

Contents

Foreword

When we met Paul Tillich for the first time on October 26, 1933, aboard the steamer "Albert Ballin," he was turning his back on Nazi Germany, and we were returning to the United States. We had taken one short sentimental journey before our departure through the Black Forest, through the Rheingau and through the Cathedral in Mainz, knowing that we would never, never encounter the same Germany again. Friends in Frankfurt am Main had told us about Paul Tillich and his family and his stand against National Socialism and asked us to assist him in finding a new home in the New World.

We went to see the Tillichs in their cabin. His wife and his little daughter Erdmutha were terribly seasick, and der Herr Professor was studying an English grammar book. We quickly agreed that I should try to teach him some English. I can still see us seriously walking around the deck, not discussing, "I am, you are, he is," but Schelling and Hegel and my true love, Goethe. Being a Lutheran, a Prussian and a judge's daughter, I was overcome with a feeling of guilt that we did not study English. So I finally said, "Let's at least translate Goethe into English." And we stood at the railing and tried:

> Füllest wieder Busch und Tal
> Still mit Nebelglanz.

And we were very homesick.

This started a long and beautiful friendship. He came year after year to visit us in Detroit, especially before World War II, and we took him to the Ford Motor Company and to concerts and to a fancy-dress ball in Ann Arbor. He had the time of his life. He always believed, like a trusting child, that my husband and I knew all the answers.

When Harold Basilius was selected to be Leo Franklin lecturer at Wayne University for the year 1953–1954 he chose as his topic, "Contemporary Problems in Religion" and asked Professor Tillich to be one of his four guest speakers. Tillich accepted immediately. He appreciated the honor and he also wished to see us again. He delivered a fine and thoughtful lecture on "Existential Analysis and Religious Symbols" which was afterwards published under Professor Basilius' editorship.

Paulus met many people at our house. He loved people and he enjoyed historians. He argued with Dr. Richard Sterba on psychoanalysis, with Professor Frank Mayer-Oakes on Japanese culture and art, with Professors Bossenbrook and Covensky on Berlin's famous Ernst Troeltsch, with Professor Goldwin Smith on the virtues of the Episcopalian Church. And he loved the young and eager students, as Hubert Locke can testify.

Paulus left us a year ago. The world is a bit emptier, a bit quieter, and we are so much poorer. The last time we saw him, he had premonitions of leaving us soon. "You were always die 'Heimat' for me," he told us, "I want to thank you for it."

We have to thank him. And I feel he would be quite astonished to know that his eminent colleagues here will hold a session on the "Intellectual Legacy of Paul Tillich."

For the truly great are the most humble.

Margaret Sterne*
October 1966
Detroit, Michigan
Wayne State University

* Editor's Note: Dr. Sterne, a close personal friend of Paul Tillich, is a professor in the History Department at Wayne State University.

Preface
The William E. Slaughter, Jr.
Foundation Lectures

In 1951, the Council of Religious Advisers at Wayne State University, representing the chaplains of the campus student religious organizations, initiated a series of discussions that led to the planning of a major campus religious center. In addition to combining program facilities for all campus religious organizations and their staffs, the center was envisioned as including facilities for the Office of Religious Affairs, a religious library, meditation room, and lecture hall. As plans for the religious center developed, the religious center board of directors turned to a group of Detroit area industrialists to advise and guide the major fund-raising program that such a project would entail. The board was extremely fortunate in securing the assistance of William E. Slaughter Jr., Vice-President of Marathon Oil Company, who led the fund-raising campaign with a gift of $25,000 designated for the religious center meditation room.

In July of 1966 ground was broken for the Charles Grosberg Religious Center which is designed as a 1.2 million-dollar complex in the six-million-dollar university center. In anticipation of this development, the Office of Religious Affairs created a number of program proposals in conjunction with the religious center, one of which called for an annual series of lectures devoted to "exploring the interrelationships between religion and modern culture." Again, through the generosity of Mr. and Mrs. Slaughter, the University has received a grant which will make possible this distinguished program. The grant, which initially has been given for the academic years 1966 through 1971, will permit the University to bring to its campus and the Detroit community outstanding scholars, both in this country and abroad, in the fields of theology, the sciences, and the humanities.

The William E. Slaughter, Jr. Lectures are under the supervision of a faculty committee and administered by the Office of Religious Affairs.

Paul Tillich

The late Paul Tillich, pastor, theologian, philosopher, and humanist, was beyond question one of the most eminent minds of the 20th century. As a professor at leading universities in both Europe and America, he was widely respected for his pioneering work in theology and philosophy, as well as for his penetrating insights in the fields of psychology and psychiatry, history, literature, and the arts.

The 1966 William E. Slaughter, Jr. Foundation Lectures have been set to coincide with the first anniversary of Professor Tillich's death. The faculty committee deemed it especially fitting that the inaugural presentation of this distinguished series of lectures deal with the intellectual con-

tribution of a scholar whose work symbolized the bridge between religion and modern culture.

I desire to express here my appreciation to H. A. Basilius for
his translation of the Tillich letter appearing in the appendix.

J. R. L.

Paul Johannes Tillich
1886-1965
Biographical Note

James R. Lyons

The late Dr. Paul Tillich was born in Prussia on August 20, 1886, the son of a Lutheran minister. He studied at the Universities of Berlin, Tübingen and Halle and received the degree doctor of philosophy from the University of Breslau in 1911. A chaplain in the German army during World War I, Dr. Tillich began his teaching career as Privatdozent in theology at the University of Berlin from 1919 to 1924. He then served successively as professor of theology at the University of Marburg (1924–25), professor of philosophy at the University of Leipzig (1925–29), and professor of philosophy at the University of Frankfurt am Main (1929–33).

An outspoken critic of Nazism, Professor Tillich became one of the first German professors compelled to leave his homeland after the rise of Hitler. In 1933 he came to America at the invitation of Union Theological Seminary. For the next twenty-two years, Dr. Tillich was professor of philosophical theology at Union. Upon his retirement in 1954 he accepted an invitation to join the faculty of the Harvard University

Divinity School and, in July of that year, Harvard President Nathan Pusey announced the appointment of Dr. Tillich as university professor at Harvard, placing him in the distinguished ranks of a small number of Harvard scholars who are free to work "on the frontiers of knowledge" without restriction to any one discipline. In September 1962, Dr. Tillich left Harvard to accept his final teaching post as John Nuveen Professor of Theology at the University of Chicago.

An author of classic works in theology, Dr. Tillich's writings have always reflected what he called his interest in the "boundary line" between theology and philosophy, as well as religion and culture. Before his death he completed the third and final volume of his life work, *Systematic Theology*, which represented, in his own words, a theology built "on the method of correlation between questions arising out of the human predicament and the answers given in the classical symbols of religion." His works in English include:

> *The Religious Situation*
> *The Interpretation of History*
> *The Protestant Era*
> *The Courage To Be*
> *Love, Power and Justice*
> *The New Being*
> *The Shaking of the Foundations*
> *Biblical Religion and the Search for Ultimate Reality*
> *Dynamics of Faith*
> *Theology of Culture*
> *Christianity and the Encounter of the World Religions*
> *The Eternal Now*
> *Morality and Beyond*

Dr. Tillich held thirteen honorary degrees from such distinguished European and American universities as Halle, Glasgow, the Free University of Berlin, Yale, Harvard, Princeton, and Chicago.

In addition he was recipient of the Goethe Medal and the Goethe Prize of the City of Frankfurt and the Grosse Verdienstkreuz, the highest service award given by the West German Republic. Dr. Tillich was married to Hannah Ulerner and had two children, a daughter and son. He died following a heart attack in Chicago on October 22, 1965.

The Philosophical Legacy
of Paul Tillich

John Herman Randall, Jr.
Columbia University

I have a great affection, as well as profound admiration and respect, for Paul Tillich. I came to hear of him when my father showed me the first of his books to be translated into English, *The Religious Situation*, which H. Richard Niebuhr put into the vernacular in 1932 (New York). This volume tried to exhibit the religious values of secularism, of the modern movements in art, science, education, and politics— the religious values actually enshrined in our modern secular culture, the culture of the nineteen-twenties. This was Tillich's first manifesto to the English-speaking world of that message which has been probably his most influential idea, the idea of his that will doubtless endure longest, that religion is not something to be confined to a single institution, the church, but rather something that must express an entire culture, and be embodied in all its institutions.

In more recent terms, Tillich was saying that our modern culture is no longer directed, as were past cultures, to a God "up there," as Bishop John Robinson has put it, as Harvey Cox has expressed it, as our "God is dead" theologians have more crudely stated it. Our culture is trying to be self-sufficient—to get along without any religious expression at all. Tillich was convinced it should see all its forms as really expressions of our human "ultimate concern." In Tillich's own technical language, our culture has ceased to be "heteronomous"—deriving its law from on high. It is at the moment trying to be "autonomous"—finding its law in itself. He went on to argue that it should endeavor to become "theonomous"—to find its law in its genuine "ultimate concern," the divine.

I came to know Tillich almost as soon as he arrived at Union Theological Seminary in 1934 as, he liked to boast, "the first German professor to be dismissed from his position —at Frankfort—by Adolf Hitler." Thereafter for some years, till his departure for Harvard, I used to give seminars with him for the Columbia and Union students.

What delighted me about him at first was that he was a typical German Romanticist—the first true-blue specimen I had ever had the opportunity to observe closely. I remember he once surprised a group of us by remarking, "Of course I would have no interest in God if I did not consider him a part of myself." This is the strain in Romanticism that led Santayana to dub that great cultural movement as "egotism in philosophy." Tillich meant, of course, the great Romantic idea that dominated so much religious thinking and feeling throughout the nineteenth century, the notion of the "immanence" of God in man, the notion that human nature is potentially divine, whatever its actual limitations as observed. In Tillich's "existential" language, he put it, "essential man," man as he might be and ought to be, is divine, in contrast to "existential man," man as he actually is, caught in the human situation—who is definitely far from being divine.

On his arrival Tillich proceeded to set up in his apartment a kind of philosophical salon or audience, where he received a group of us Columbia philosophers together with some of his former German friends who had followed him to this country. He had formerly conducted such gatherings at Frankfort, and before long the entire group had transferred to New York. There were a number of philosophically-minded psychiatrists and depth psychologists, among whom Kurt Goldstein was the most distinguished. What Tillich's intellectual leadership meant to his friends is illustrated by the case of one of the old Frankfort colleagues, Theodor Wiesengrund-Adorno who, as Theodor Adorno, since his return to Germany in 1945, has risen high in academic circles. Adorno left the ship at five p.m., and at seven-thirty was with the group at Tillich's, continuing the familiar Frankfort association.

Tillich also joined a club of American philosophers meeting in New York and drawn from universities as far away as Hopkins. On one occasion he read a brilliant paper on "Existential Philosophy" (reprinted in *The Theology of Culture*, Robert C. Kimball, Ed., Oxford 1959). Among the listeners was G. E. Moore, the distinguished representative of a very different philosophical tradition and language. When it came time for Moore to comment on Tillich's paper, he said, "Now really, Mr. Tillich, I don't think I have been able to understand a single sentence of your paper. Won't you please try to state one sentence, or even one word, that I can understand?" Moore's failure to comprehend was professional, and Tillich is clearly no Cambridge analyst.

On another occasion a group of us were discussing that philosophical movement with John Dewey. Dewey remarked, "Well, I have had some pretty hard things to say about German philosophers in my time. But at least they were dealing with the important questions." I do not think any philosophical mind can have talked with or read Tillich without being profoundly convinced that he was dealing with the important questions. To be sure, Moore had a point, which Tillich freely granted. Like most recent German philosophers —and older ones as well—Tillich could profitably have cultivated a little more precision of definition. But it was the one systematic philosopher to have come out of the Cambridge tradition in the last generation, Alfred North Whitehead, who exclaimed in understandable if not entirely accurate revulsion, "Exactness is a fake!" The precise statement of nothing of consequence is surely specious, and the meaning of human destiny can scarcely be cramped within the bounds of symbolic logic or of ordinary language.

An important part of my personal experience with Paul Tillich was in connection with the editing for publication of certain of his papers, including the one read on the abovementioned occasion. Tillich was most anxious to get his originally rather Teutonic style into the English—or the American—philosophic tongue. Patiently he listened to my fumbling efforts to translate his thought into the vernacular, and he eagerly tried to incorporate my suggestions. Above all he wanted to be understood, to reach those immune to the language of traditional theology—or of German philosophy.

The same endeavor dominated our joint seminars. He made every effort to understand what I was trying to say in my language, and to come to terms with the American philosophizing I was trying to enunciate, so that he could put what he had to give in terms that would be understood by American students. Mostly we conducted seminars on the theme, "Myths and Symbols." Once we tried "The human situation"—or, as we agreed on putting it, "The fix in which man finds himself." That seminar started with some hundred and sixty members, a little large for a working seminar. But so convinced were the students that Paul Tillich had something to tell them that it grew larger and larger with every meeting.

Paul Tillich was essentially a master of what I should call "philosophical theology." That is, he was trying to interpret the Christian faith in terms of our present-day philosophic ways of understanding the world and man's place in it. Like his contemporary Rudolf Bultmann, he believed in "demythologization," in freeing that faith from the mythical beliefs in terms of which it had been first formulated, and to which the great theologians of the early church had added a large store. But Tillich differed from Bultmann in that he did not want simply to get rid of the myths, he rather wanted to retain them but to recognize them as what they were, myths and symbols whose meaning had to be elucidated. But for both Bultmann and Tillich, what was left when the myths were removed, or what they were interpreted as symbolizing, was a version of the existential philosophy as a literal and contemporary way of understanding the world.

Tillich was indeed a philosophical theologian. The Christian faith—the central significance of the event in which Christianity was born—had from the beginning, he held, been expressed in religious symbols which have required continual reinterpretation. "The way in which this event can be understood and received changes with changing conditions in all periods of history."[1] For large groups of the educated today, "the traditional language has become irrelevant," and the meaning of the Christian symbols has become increasingly problematic. That meaning—the eternal message of the Christ—must today be interpreted with the language, the conceptual tools, that are expressions of our own culture.

This is the enterprise Tillich attempted in the final statement of his thought, his *Systematic Theology*, on which he had been working since the twenties. It involves employing current philosophical and psychological concepts, and coming to terms with current sociological and scientific theories. This is the traditional task of philosophical theology. Such a task presupposes some common ground between the questions our culture is asking, or ought to be asking, in its own novel ways, and the answers that can be found in the Christian symbols, properly interpreted. This common ground Tillich locates in the fact that, while the questions must be formulated in the language and concepts of today's situation, the questions themselves are those implied in the universal human situation—in the human "predicament." And it is precisely these eternal questions to which the Christian message and symbols have always given an answer.

In the enterprise of philosophical theology, the Christian symbols can always be given some meaning in terms of the reigning way of understanding human life in the world. Again and again the will of man has been able to turn the trick. "Theology is always possible on the basis of any philosophical tradition."[2] Each of the successive major schemes of understanding developed in the Western tradition has been employed to give a new interpretation to the symbols of faith. The question has always been, "Can the Christian message be adapted to the modern mind without losing its essential and unique character?"[3] In these past attempts, the results have always been "ambiguous." Normally, the answers themselves have been derived from the questions: they have been furnished by the scheme of understanding employed to formulate the needs and values of a specific historical situation. The Christian symbols have been identified with the first principles of that inevitably limited scheme of intelligibility. In the process of bringing the Christian message into the contemporary situation, the message has been dissolved. It has never been completely obliterated; the principles of any philosophical theology remain the expressions of an ultimate concern. But the meaning of the symbols has been confined within the limits of what the situation could understand, receive and assimilate.

To remedy this defect of philosophical theology, Tillich proposed what he called the "method of correlation." The originality of this method, he thought, lies in its awareness of this "ambiguity" of philosophical theology and in its effort to avoid the sacrifice of the power and fullness of religious symbols to the limitations of philosophical concepts. In his method of correlation he confines the philosophical formulation to the analysis of the human situation and the statement of the questions it suggests. The theological answer "implied" in the message is "independent" of the questions asked, but is "correlated" with them. "One cannot derive a divine self-manifestation from an analysis of the human predicament."[4] His method rather "correlates questions and answers, situation and message, human existence and divine manifestation."[5] Philosophy asks the questions, theology uses religious symbols to answer them. The questions are formulated independently, the answers are not reduced to the compass of the concepts in which the questions are stated, but are given independently in the revelatory message.*

* Paul Tillich here contends that philosophers raise problems, stated in the language of philosophy, which only theologians can solve, in the language of theology. I should say myself, on the contrary, that theologians raise problems, stated in what they try to make the language of philosophy, which can only be solved by philosophers willing to talk in the language of theology. If one wants to talk in a non-literal language, which deals with philosophical issues in terms of non-existent entities, I submit, the "language of theology" is far superior to the "language of linguistic analysis," the language of non-existent "sense-data," and of non-existent "common usage"; it can deal with a far wider range of philosophical problems.

But the situation does not seem to be actually quite so simple as Tillich presents it: it is rather highly "dialectical." Questions and answers are in some respects independent of each other, but in other respects, Tillich admits, they are "interdependent" and mutually dependent. Correlation means, in fact, "interdependence of two independent factors."[6] First, for theology to provide the answers, philosophy has to ask the right questions, "The revelatory answer is meaningless if there is no question to which it is the answer. Man cannot receive an answer to a question he has not asked." The philosopher must be "existentially" involved in the human predicament; he must be seeking a solution to the ambiguities and conflicts of man's existential situation; he must ask the "existential" questions. He must as a "hidden theologian" be asking the questions about man's ultimate concern which can be answered not by philosophy but by theology. In short, for a religious message—"the self-manifestation of the divine"—to provide in its symbols a significant answer, the questions must themselves be religious, and specifically such that those symbols will be felt as significant answers. What questions can be answered depends on the answers available.

Secondly, in showing his religious answers to be significant, the theologian is deeply involved in determining the questions themselves. From the whole of human experience in its manifold expression he selects just those aspects, just that material, that reflects man's "existential predicament," and that is needed to formulate the "existential questions" whose religious answer he has found. The organization and pointing up of this material, the very raising of the questions, belong to the theologian. "The choice of the material, as well as the formulation of the question, is the task of the systematic theologian."[7]

Thirdly, the theological answers dictate the precise way in which the questions will be put. "The form of the question is determined by the total system and by the answers given in it. The question implied in human finitude is directed toward the answer: the eternal. The question implied in human estrangement is directed toward the answer: forgiveness." How man is to be saved determines the precise character of what he needs to be saved from.

On the other hand, the way in which the questions are formulated and put has in turn a profound influence on the way the answers are taken and understood. "The form of the theological answer is *not* independent of the form of the existential question." If "the Christ" is given as the answer to human estrangement, that answer will be stated and understood differently, "depending on whether the reference is to the existential conflicts of Jewish legalism, to the existential despair of Greek Skepticism, or to the threat of nihilism as expressed in twentieth-century literature, art, and psychology." The question does not indeed create the answer. "The answer, 'the Christ,' cannot be created by man, but man can receive it and express it according to the way he has asked for it."[8] A question formulated in one language and set of concepts will naturally receive an answer that will be understood in those terms. For the meaning of an answer depends on the question to which it is an answer.

If, then, both the material and the form of the questions raised philosophically about man are determined by the answers the theologian can give, and if those answers themselves, the meanings of religious symbols, are received and understood in terms of the cultural situation in which the questions are asked, it is a little difficult to see the precise way in which questions and answers are "independent" of each other, or in which Tillich has escaped the ambiguities of previous systems of philosophical theology. He is still trying, like Hegel, or like Henry Nelson Wieman in our own day, to interpret the Christian symbols in terms of one of the schemes of philosophical understanding popular in his own time, and is thus involved in all the ambiguities and paradoxes to which such an enterprise is subject. The "method of correlation" hardly seems significantly different from the method of previous philosophical theologians. And Tillich in the end freely admits as much. "As method, it is as old as theology. We have therefore not admitted a new method, but have rather tried to make explicit the implications of the old one, namely, that of apologetic theology."[9]

Concretely, of course, the philosophical scheme of understanding on which Tillich relies to interpret the meaning of the Christian symbols is his own version of the existentialist philosophy. That philosophy he sees beginning in recent times with the revolt of the later Schelling, of Kierkegaard, and of the early Marx against Hegel and his "perfect essentialism"—his conviction that the world and man have been realizing their potentialities in the world process, that "existence is the expression of essence and not the fall away from it." Existentialists, rebelling against "the self-interpretation of man in modern industrial society," all insist that "man's existential situation is a state of estrangement from his essential nature." Tillich's own version of existentialism concentrates upon the analysis of this "existential" state of man, upon the human predicament. For the existentialist revolt has helped to rediscover "the classical Christian interpretation of human existence," as symbolized in the myth of the Fall, which Tillich reads in the half-mythical form of "the transition from essence to existence." Existentialism is thus a natural ally of Christianity, for it has rediscovered the truth about man's predicament lost during the optimistic early modern period; together existentialism and Christianity should analyze the character of man's existence or actuality.

Tillich does not restrict existentialism to a philosophical movement; he finds its analysis of the human situation to be "the cultural self-expression of the Western world in the twentieth century." Indeed, "the most striking existentialist analyses have been made by novelists, poets, and painters," like Dostoevsky, Rilke, or Kafka. The theologian must draw on materials furnished by these creative representatives of existentialism in all realms of culture; he must learn from the practical explorers of man's predicament, from ministers and educators; he must use the results of the detached methods of therapeutic depth psychology.

For Tillich, existentialism thus gives an analysis of what it means to "exist," of what actual human life is like. It does not try to give the answers, to tell what man must do to be saved. The more philosophical minds who have made that attempt have done so in terms of religious or quasi-religious traditions not derived from their existential analysis, even the humanists, who have drawn on "hidden religious sources." For "the answers to the questions implied in man's predicament are religious, whether open or hidden." Tillich the theologian prefers to find the answers in the symbols of the Christian message.

Tillich's philosophical theology is thus the interpretation of the Christian symbols in terms of his own particular philosophy of Christian existentialism. That he should have been extraordinarily successful in translating their meaning into existentialist concepts, that he should have been able to achieve a remarkable consistency, and to contruct a "system" impressive in its wholeness, exhibiting a rich and fruitful complex of dynamic interrelations, is hardly surprising. For it is not merely a matter of "good luck"[10] that existentialism should prove to be so admirable an instrument for the philosophical exploration and expression of Christian theology. From its beginning in Kierkegaard and the later Schelling it was intended to be just that. It sprang from a reaffirmation of the classical Christian vision of the ambiguities of human nature, and in the later Schelling, so influential in moulding Tillich's ontology, it tried to conceive Being in such a way as to explain the human situation and to provide the background for the Christian scheme of salvation. All forms of existentialism, as Tillich shows, ask the Christian questions; many later and recent versions give other and non-Christian answers, but they too set out on the same quest. In working out the meaning of the Christian answers, Tillich is thus with consummate skill realizing the essential function of existentialism, to furnish the concepts for a Christian philosophical theology. It is little wonder he impatiently brushes aside the many other philosophical expressions of our culture as irrelevant, or as at best of subsidiary value. He may be deviating from traditional biblical or ecclesiastical language, like all philosophical theologians, but he is employing a philosophical language definitely worked out to deal with the fundamental issues of Christian theology. That is why he can treat those issues so effectively, and why he can bring home their relevance to the cultural problems of today. Previous philosophical theologies often relied on philosophical concepts originally directed to other and frequently irrelevant ends—as when St. Thomas used Aristotle's scientific philosophy to interpret the Christian message. Tillich's aim is concentrated as few previously on man and his religious needs and concerns.

When we turn to Tillich's philosophy itself, we find it profoundly influenced by the university training he received. At Halle the young theologian's son was greatly attracted by

Martin Kähler's lectures on theology, and by those of Fritz Medicus on philosophy. Medicus introduced him to classical German Idealism—Medicus was expert on Fichte in particular, and had edited his works. Tillich found a chance bargain of a complete set of Schelling in a bookstore, which he read through; this introduced him to the thought of the German philosopher he ever after found most congenial and suggestive, especially the writings of Schelling's later or "positive" period. Both Tillich's dissertations were on Schelling,[11] who ever after largely determined Tillich's views on ontology. Saturated in German philosophical Idealism, Tillich found an exciting colleague at Marburg, Martin Heidegger. He was impressed by Heidegger's profound influence on his students, and finished absorbing from him the existentialist criticisms of Idealism his reading and his war experience as chaplain on the Western front had already led him to take seriously. Heidegger's atheism at that time of course had no appeal.

Thus the immediate background of Tillich's philosophy is the German Idealistic tradition, especially as found in the later or "positive" philosophy of Schelling, as reconstructed in certain of the more ontological and historical strains of the nineteenth-century German criticism of the Idealists. The post-Böhme thought of Schelling, the various mid-century reactions against the panlogism of Hegel, like those of Feuerbach and the early Marx of the "Economic and Philosophical Manuscripts of 1844," which Tillich always took very seriously after their publication in 1932, of Nietzsche and the "philosophy of life," and of the more recent post-Heideggerian existentialism—all these contributed to his formulation of philosophic issues and problems. In particular, they furnished him with a large part of the philosophical vocabulary with which he talked about the world and about earlier attempts to understand it. To express his own insights, Tillich employs the language of the existential philosophy of the last generation on the continent. Whether this is the best possible language to put what he had to say is immaterial. Certainly he greatly modified and clarified it after coming to America, for he discovered it to be a real barrier to American understanding of his thought. It is obviously a language not too familiar to the vernacular of most American philosophizing in this century, and hardly one with which English-speaking theologians had grown up. This circumstance has created a problem of communication, of which Tillich himself was always keenly aware, which has not been lessened by the recent American shift to the language of English analysis.

More fundamentally, however, both as philosopher and as theologian Tillich stands broadly in the great Augustinian tradition, like any confirmed Lutheran—that is, in the central tradition of Christian Platonism. For him, the lesson of the *Symposium* has been well learned: knowledge is ultimately a "participation" in true Being.[12] This is what existentialism meant for him intellectually. Immediately, as with Heidegger, this is a protest against the "bracketing" of questions of existence, and against the exclusive concern with a description of essences, that was characteristic of the early phenomenological analysis of Edmund Husserl, the most important philosophical movement in the Germany in which Tillich grew up. But more ultimately for Tillich the concern with "existence" is a reaffirmation of the Platonic doctrine of *eros* and participation. Historically speaking, this sets Tillich against the Thomistic natural theology which recognizes a clear boundary between the realm of truths accessible to "natural reason" and the realm of truths accessible only to faith, and for him renders any natural theology—like the many developed by nineteenth and twentieth-century religious liberals—

strictly impossible.[13] It sets him against the Aristotle who made science an integral part of wisdom: he found only the Platonic strain in Aristotle congenial.

And so Tillich stands in the great tradition of Augustinian philosophy; his relation to the intricacies of Augustinian and Lutheran theology is more complex. This is a way of saying that on certain crucial questions, particularly of epistemology and ontology, his thought differs from the equally great tradition of Christian Aristotelianism. For him, it was with St. Thomas Aquinas that the course of Christian thought went astray. He recognizes no neat line dividing philosophy from theology. In a real sense, for Tillich philosophy is "faith seeking understanding"—though "faith" appears in him as "existential commitment." For him there can be no natural theology: any argument from the character of the world to the "existence" of God could never hope to get beyond finite relativities; and "God" is not "a being" whose "existence" demands proof. Tillich rests upon a version of the ontological argument—or rather, as for all true Augustinians, God—that is, that Ultimate in which the symbols that are human ideas of "God" participate, which neither needs nor can receive "proof." For that Ultimate—Tillich's term is Schelling's *das Unbedingte*, the Unconditioned—is a certain quality or "dimension" of the world man encounters, which analysis reveals as "presupposed" in all man's encountering. Whereas Augustine's Platonism, however, led him to an intellectual emphasis on the Truth or Logos implied in all knowledge, Tillich expanded the Ultimate to "the Power of Being" implied in all men's varied participations in the world in which they are "grasped by an ultimate concern."

Now all this can mean much or little, depending on how it is elaborated. As Tillich developed it, it becomes a suggestive reinterpretation of the Augustinian metaphysics, fertilized with many of the insights of over a century of German thinking. Largely—though not wholly freed from the epistemological entanglements in which classic German Idealism had mired Christian Platonism, Tillich's philosophy is a realistic interpretation of a world in which man can find a meaning for his life. Some of the doubts it leaves in the mind of a sympathetic seeker for wisdom arise from the baggage it carries along from a century of German philosophical engagements. Others are probably inherent in the Christian and Augustinian character of its Platonism, when viewed from the perspective of either an Aristotelian or a modern empirical approach. But it is not Tillich's central enterprise with which I should want to quarrel: the working-out of a realism with vision and "participation"—what he used to call a "belief-full or self-transcending realism."[14]

The three main points in this philosophy are the nature of philosophy itself, the nature of reason, and the nature of Being. Here I shall comment on the first two; the third is too technical, and would lead too far into the intricacies of Tillich's ontology.

Philosophy Tillich defines as "that cognitive approach to reality in which reality as such is the object. Reality as such, or reality as a whole, is not the whole of reality; it is the structure which makes reality a whole and therefore a potential object of knowledge."[15] These structures, of course, *pace* the Kantians and the positivists, include structures of values. Now philosophy deals with the structures of Being in itself: it undertakes an ontological analysis of those structures. Theology deals with the *meaning* of Being *for us*. Consequently the two diverge, first, in their cognitive attitude. "The philosopher tries to maintain a detached objectivity toward Being and its structures. He tries to exclude the personal, social, and historical conditions which might distort an objective vision of reality."[16] In contrast, the basic attitude of the theologian is commitment to the content he expounds, is "existential." Secondly, the two differ in that the philosopher like the scientist is seeking a universal structure, the theologian a structure manifesting itself in a particular historical event and religious institution. Thirdly, the philosopher deals with the categories of Being in relation to the material which is structured by them, while the theologian treats them in relation to the salvation of man.

Actually, of course, the philosopher too is conditioned by his psychological, sociological, and historical situation, and if he be of any significance has his own "ultimate concern." His existential situation and his ultimate concern shape his philosophical vision. To the extent that this is true, the philosopher is also by definition a theologian, as all creative philosophers are. He tries to become universal, but he is destined to remain particular.

Two points here require comment. The first is Tillich's definition of the core of philosophy, ontology. He passes easily from "Being as such" to "reality as a whole," identifying two very different conceptions of ontology. The first is Aristotelian, the second is the object of nineteenth-century Idealism. The "structure of Being" thus means for Tillich two different things. The first is the proper object of an Aristotelian ontological inquiry; the second is the goal of Platonic and Neoplatonic aspiration, the "Being" that is the Idea of the Good and The One, which Christian tradition has always identified with "God."

To me, this second idea seems to have been, in the whole Platonic tradition, one of those great unifying symbols or "myths" by which men bring their encountered world to a focus in terms of their system of meanings and values—of their "ultimate concern." It is a symbol by which the world manages to unify itself. I should say, it is part of the task of metaphysics or ontology to *understand* such myths and the way they function. It is a part of the task of "practical" philosophy (and I should here include philosophical theology, as well as the philosophy of history) to *use* such myths for the direction of human life, to clarify and to criticize them. Speaking as a metaphysician, it seems to me important to recognize that "reality as a whole" has the ontological status of a myth or symbol, rather than that of a descriptive hypothesis. In Kantian terms it is a "regulative idea." It is, in Tillich's own distinction, an "existential" rather than a theoretical concept.

This brings us to the second point about Tillich's conception of the nature of philosophy. As an Augustinian he finds it ultimately impossible to set philosophy apart from theology, and his efforts to distinguish their two different emphases of course in the last analysis break down. The distinction is relative and "existential"—it depends on the specific situation. Now I have no particular objection to calling all the concern of the philosophical enterprise with "practice" and values really "theology," as Tillich does in his broadest extension of that discipline—the sense in which a teacup by Cezanne is a revelation of "Being" and of man's ultimate concern. To do so makes aesthetics and indeed all reflection on man's cultural institutions branches of theology.*

* It is this broad sense of theology Tillich has in mind in setting forth his conception of the "theology of culture," which deals with the "religious dimension" of all men's creative cultural activities—the way in which they all express man's "ultimate concern," even if they are not "religious" in the narrower sense. See the early "Ueber die Idee einer Theologie der Kultur," in G. Radbruch und Paul Tillich, *Religionsphilosophie der Kultur* (1919). Here belong Tillich's penetrating treatments of art and of psychoanalysis.

The root difficulty in all these distinctions seems to lie in the too-sharp dualism Tillich accepts between the theoretical and the existential or "practical." It has been one of the major contributions of the broad philosophical movement, of which both existentialism and American "instrumentalism" are strands, to break down this dualism, which goes back through Kant to Aristotle. The theoretical interest, or "pure reason," it has been abundantly shown, is not something *opposed* to the practical or existential. Rather, theory and detached objectivity are moments or *stages* in a broader context or matrix of "practice." Different sciences and disciplines vary in the degree to which they attain universality and detachment; metaphysics, in seeking to embrace all possible situations, can hope to become the most "theoretical" of all and hence at the same time the most "instrumental" and "existential." Tillich accepts all this, but there seems still a strong remnant of the Kantial dualism left in the way he uses this distinction. This comes out clearly in his final position on the relation between philosophy and theology, in his so-called "method of correlation," in which he finds that philosophy must go to theology for the answers to its own questions. Unless this be a mere matter of terminology, it clearly does not take the "existential" character of all theory seriously enough.

Just as Tillich develops his conception of philosophy as a preparation for theology, so he analyzes *reason* to lead up to the reality of revelation. He starts by distinguishing two conceptions of reason, the "ontological" and the "technical" —νοῦς or *intellectus,* and διάνοια or *ratio.* "According to the classical philosophical tradition, reason is the structure of the mind which enables the mind to grasp and transform reality . . . Classical reason is Logos, whether it is understood in a more intuitive or in a more critical way. Its cognitive nature is one element in addition to others; it is cognitive and aesthetic, theoretical and practical, detached and passionate, subjective and objective."[17]

Technical reason is the capacity for reasoning. It is Aristotle's "deliberative reason," which calculates means to ends. Ontological reason, *Vernunft*, is capable both of participating in the universal Logos of Being, and of succumbing to the destructive structures of existence. It is partly liberated from blindness, and partly held in it. In Platonic terms it can either turn upward to participate in true Being, or turn downward to non-being. It is itself both subjective and objective; the human logos can grasp and shape reality only because reality itself has a logos character. To the rational structure of the mind there corresponds an intelligible structure of the world. Subjective reason both "grasps" and "shapes": the mind receives and reacts. Ontological reason has a dimension which Tillich calls "depth." "The depth of reason is the expression of something that is not reason but which precedes reason and is manifest through it. Reason in both its objective and subjective structures points to something which appears in these structures but which transcends them in power and meaning."[18]

Reason, in other words, points to something that is one step beyond the intelligible structures it actually finds. This further step is the Source or The One of Neoplatonism, the Imprinter of the seal, the Original of the copy, of the Augustinian metaphors. For the Platonic tradition this stands one step "above" intellect and νοῦς; following Böhme and Schelling, Tillich locates it rather one step "below," in "the depths." It is the Standard by which finite, human intellectual activity ultimately judges. But though it thus manifests itself in every act of reason, it is there hidden under the conditions of existence, and expresses itself primarily in myth and in ritual. "Myth is not primitive science, nor is cult primitive morality. Their content, as well as the attitude of people toward them, discloses elements which transcend science as well as morality—elements of infinity which express ultimate concern."[19]

When Tillich comes to consider the cognitive function of ontological reason, and the nature of human knowledge, "cognitive reason under the conditions of existence," he emphasizes its basic polar structure. Knowledge he takes, with the Platonic tradition, to be a form of union. "In every act of knowledge the knower and that which is known are united." But knowledge is a union through detachment and separation: in every type of knowledge subject and object are logically distinguished.

Union and detachment or estrangement are thus present in all knowledge. But there are two major types, that in which detachment is determining, and that in which union is predominant. The first type Tillich, following Max Scheler, calls "controlling knowledge." This is the product of technical, instrumental reason. "It unites subject and object for the sake of the control of the object by the subject. It transforms the object into a completely conditioned and calculable 'thing.' It deprives it of any subjective quality."[20] But this is not the way of knowing human nature, or any individual personality. "Without union there is no cognitive approach to man." The type of knowledge where union predominates Tillich calls "receiving knowledge." It always includes the emotional element: no union of subject and object is possible without emotional participation. Knowledge in which there is a balance of union and detachment is "understanding." "Understanding another person or a historical figure, the life of an animal or a religious text, involves an amalgamation of controlling and receiving knowledge, of union and detachment, of participation and analysis."[21]

Modern culture has seen a tidal wave of "controlling knowledge," of technical reason, which has swamped every cognitive attempt in which "reception" and union are presupposed. "Man actually has become what controlling knowledge considers him to be, a thing among things, a cog in the dominating machine of production and consumption, a dehumanized object of tyranny or a standardized object of public communication."[22]

Three main movements have protested against this outcome: Romanticism, the *Lebensphilosophie* or "philosophy of life," and existentialism. They have all failed because they had no adequate criterion of truth and falsity. What does "truth" mean for "receiving knowledge"? Positivists would restrict the term to either tautologies or experimentally confirmed sentences. But this involves a break with the whole classic tradition. Modern philosophy, following Aristotle, has taken "true" as a quality of judgments. Tillich protests by asserting the ancient Platonic and Augustinian position, that the truth of judgments depends on a prior "truth" in things themselves. "The truth of something is that level of its being the knowledge of which prevents wrong expectations and consequent disappointments."[23] This would have delighted St. Anselm.

Tillich is obviously committed to finding a method of verification for his "receiving knowledge" that is different from that of experimental science. "It is not permissible to make the experimental method of verification the exclusive pattern of all verification . . . The verifying experiences of a non-experimental character are truer to life, though less exact and definite. By far the largest part of all cognitive verification is 'experiential'. . . . Controlling knowledge is verified by the success of controlling actions. . . . Receiving knowledge is verified by the creative union of two natures, that of knowing, and that of the known. This test, of course, is neither repeatable, precise, or final at any particular moment. The life-process itself makes the test. . . . There is an element of risk connected with it. . . . Experiential verification must go on continually, whether it is supported by experimental tests or not."[24]

This suggests that in most of those traits in which the knowledge gained by experimental science has been contrasted unfavorably with knowledge gained by more "certain" methods, "receiving knowledge" is far more "experimental" than "controlling knowledge." It is more tentative, less precise, more subject to reconstruction with further experience. Such knowledge is "verified partly by experimental tests, partly by a participation in the individual life with which they deal. If this 'knowledge by participation' is called 'intuition,' the cognitive approach to every individual life-process is intuitive. Intuition in this sense is not irrational, and neither does it by-pass a full consciousness of experimentally verified knowledge."[25]

Now neither rationalism nor pragmatism sees the element of participation in reason. But the way in which philosophical systems have been accepted, experienced, and verified points to a method of verification beyond rationalism or pragmatism. In terms of controlling knowledge, rational criticism, or pragmatic tests, they have been refuted innumerable times. But they continue to live. Their verification is their efficacy in the life-process of mankind. They prove to be inexhaustible in meaning and creative power. This method of verification "somehow combines the pragmatic and the rational elements without falling into the fallacies of either pragmatism or rationalism."[26]

Now, Tillich's fundamental logical realism—the notion of an "objective" intelligible structure which is grasped by "subjective" human reason—is designedly not in the fashion of much recent nominalistic philosophizing. In this, Tillich is not only in the classic tradition of ontology; he is, I judge, on the side of the angels—of the cherubim who *know* God. And it is to be criticized only at those points where he inadvertently allows Kantian epistemology to interfere with it. The difficulties in the working-out of such a realism he does not face. They are, I judge, to be met only in a thoroughly functional realism; and Tillich remains with a purely structural realism. He defines reason as "the structure of the mind," instead of as "the power of the mind" to operate in the ways it ascertainably does.

That the mind has the power—or, more precisely, *is* the power—to do what he assigns to "ontological reason," as well as what he calls "technical reason," is undoubtedly true. Tillich himself is inclined to stop short with these facts, rather than to pursue the analysis of what is a much more complex process than he often suggests. Perhaps this is sufficient for his purposes as a theologian. Reason can and does determine ends as well as means, but hardly in the simple sense of the Platonic tradition, of participating in them intuitively as he himself goes on to illustrate. There are overtones of the Greek νοῦς and the Idealistic *Vernunft*, as well as of the Christian Logos, that at times obscure what he is really trying to point to.

That mind has and is the power of "depth" no sensitive man would care to deny, with the capacity for envisaging more ultimate perfections than man can actually achieve. That the powers of the mind are limited is likewise obvious, and the polarities and tensions Tillich points to are both historically and personally illuminating. The limitations of what he calls an "autonomous reason" that disregards its "depth" have not been exactly overlooked of late; sensitivity to other aspects of experience is certainly needed. The higher autonomy Tillich calls "theonomy": if this be one way of defining "God" it is surely as good as any other. The polar values of both relativism and absolutism are equally obvious. That this is a rationally insoluble antinomy, however, is by no means clear. The solution would seem to lie in an objective relativism, a position Tillich does not consider. Even if he be right in contending that "only that which is absolute and concrete at the same time" can solve the antinomy, this still seems to be a rational answer to a rational question, and not beyond the power of reason, however difficult practically. Finally, the antinomy between formalism and emotionalism seems likewise capable of rational adjustment. In going beyond the traditional "technical reason" to the notion of "intelligence," recent philosophizing has been facing and dealing with precisely this problem.

In other words, the finite and relative character of human reason is clear, as well as the fact that it confronts difficulties and "ambiguities." That any adequate intellectual method, however, faces ultimate self-contradiction, Tillich has hardly established. He contends that only "revelation" can solve these contradictions. Now there is no objection to calling the power of reason to solve its difficulties "revelation," especially if the power be seen as a cooperation of man with the powers of the world to be intelligible—if "revelation" be taken as a discovery and not as a mere human invention. That only the Christian "revelation" can solve the problems, however, is another matter again. That particular revelation, philosophically considered, would be one hypothesis among others, and would have to be tested philosophically. "Revelation," that is, would seem to be a symbol for a power of reason to do what revelation notoriously does.

In treating the nature of knowledge, Tillich does not presume to offer a detailed epistemology. His distinctions are important; his language is obviously loaded in the direction of establishing theological "knowledge." But though he has the tradition on his side, there remains a doubt whether greater clarity would not come from calling his "receiving knowledge" by some other name than "knowledge." After all, it is only by a metaphor that knowledge can be called a "union" or a "participation." "Love" for the object of knowledge may in many types of knowledge be essential for any real "understanding"; but does that make the love itself knowledge? "Knowing is not like digesting, and we do not devour what we mean," is an aphorism of Santayana's still worth pondering. "Union" with another personality may well be a necessary condition of adequate knowledge of that personality. But union with a text, even with a religious text, is hardly necessary to its proper interpretation. Nor have many American students been able to accept the peculiar German view of historical knowledge which leads Tillich to say, "Without a union of the nature of the historian with that of his object, no significant history is possible." In what sense, for example, does a significant history of capitalism demand "a union between the nature of the historian and the nature of" capitalism? Obviously, only by metaphor.

This may be a mere matter of terminology, and there is of course plenty of precedent for identifying forms of immediate experience with "knowledge." Precedent, however, is hardly a philosophical justification. The knowledge of particular situations does involve a very complex gathering together of relevant factors, as well as a narrowly "technical" reason. The classic instance is the process of diagnosis in medicine. But the physician scarcely needs to be "united" with the disease. To strengthen his particular kind of "receiving knowledge," Tillich seems to have grouped together quite a variety of types of knowledge that in another connection would demand careful discrimination.

It is obvious that most of our so-called "knowledge" is verified "experientially," rather than "experimentally" at least in the narrow laboratory sense. But like most Idealists criticizing philosophies of "scientific method," Tillich in the end falls back, in language quite worthy of William James himself, on a pretty crude pragmatic method of verification, "efficacy in the life-process of mankind." Actually, of course, what he carefully describes as a union of experimental verification with something more, and calls both an "experiential" and an "intuitive" method, is very close to what Americans, pragmatists and instrumentalists and others, have called "the method of intelligence." It is natural for those without scientific interests themselves to conceive "scientific method" very narrowly, to identify it with what Tillich calls "technical reason." But "intelligence," as the best American philosophic thought has conceived it, is certainly far more than his "technical reason" even if it has still to learn some of the "depth" of his "ontological reason." Tillich would really have done well to strike up an acquaintance with "intelligence." He might in the end even have been willing to participate in it.

We have been considering Tillich's interpretation of the Christian symbols in terms of Schellingian and existentialist concepts.* To these Tillich adds still another set of concepts.

---

* For a detailed analysis of Tillich's ideas on ontology and the structures of Being, see J. H. Randall, Jr., "The Ontology of Paul Tillich," in *The Theology of Paul Tillich,* ed. Charles W. Kegley and Robert W. Bretall (New York, 1952), pp. 151–61. Another important strand of Tillich's philosophic thought, his philosophic interpretation of history, is also left unconsidered here, especially his suggestive view of "the center of history."

Since the Holy Spirit is the presence of God in life, he sets forth his own version of *Lebensphilosophie,* that view which takes "life" as of universal scope, as the name for any "actuality of Being" whatever. All finite beings are the actualization of certain potentialities, and it is this universal process of actualization which is "life"; the notion of "life" is thus broadened to include the inorganic as well, since that too enjoys a potential participation in all the higher realms of being. This view that the whole world-process is in fact a realization of the *unbewusster Geist* coming to consciousness in man is of course the key idea in Schelling's earliest philosophy, his Philosophy of Nature.

Tillich dislikes the notion of ontological "levels," as developed by Nicolai Hartmann, for example, which he identifies with the Neoplatonic hierarchical order of realms of being. He prefers the metaphor of "dimension," since dimensions do not conflict with each other, and since all dimensions can be found, at least potentially, in all "realms." Actually, Tillich too has a scale or order of "conditioning": "The appearance of a new dimension of life is dependent on a constellation of conditions in the conditioning dimension."[27] All the "preceding" dimensions in the scale are necessary conditions of the new one, which as including them all is "richer" and "higher." Tillich distinguishes on his scale the inorganic, the organic, the psychological (marked by "inner awareness"), "spirit" *(Geist),* and the historical. Each dimension is set off by exhibiting its own unique categorial structures: for each there is its own distinctive form of time, space, causation, and substance.

The peculiarly human dimension is "spirit." Tillich identifies it with "the personal-communal," the "unity of power and meaning," and finds it in the achievement of a "centered self," the necessary condition of moral and cognitive acts.

This is the personal self that deliberates and makes decisions in freedom, and that knows. He seems to think of this self in terms of Kant's transcendental unity of apperception. The relation between this "centered self" and the "constellation of psychological factors" out of which it "leaps" illustrates the general relation between any higher dimension of "life" and the next "lower" one. This personal self presupposes and is conditioned by its psychological materials, but transcends them. It is not identical with any psychological content, nor is it an additional such element. It actualizes itself by knowing or by deciding in the total response that is human freedom, in polar opposition to the conditioning materials that represent its human destiny. In so acting it actualizes the dimension of "spirit." Thus there is neither a dualism between spirit and the psychological, nor is spirit reduced to the psychological out of which it arises. Thus Tillich tries to avoid both dualism and psychological monism.

Whether he has actually succeeded here in doing more than restate the central problem in any scheme of emergent levels or dimensions, the problem of the precise relation between the levels remains an open question. At least his "multidimensional unity of life" emphasizes the essential unity of human nature in all its manifold dimensions. New dimensions achieved add to, they do not remove, the earlier ones and the conditioning they impose on the higher dimension. Thus the inorganic is the "first condition" for the actualization of all the higher dimensions; the psychological is the necessary condition for the freedom of "spirit," which can never escape that psychological conditioning, though it can "transcend" it. On the other hand, even the inorganic has the potentiality of realizing in itself the dimension of spirit. There are strong echoes here of Schelling's "unconscious spirit" *(unbewusster Geist)*. Tillich rejects all forms of reductionist ontology, both naturalistic and Idealistic, for a scale of levels or dimensions of being that proceed to incorporate more and more dimensions. As we ascend the scale, even the categories of Being are enlarged rather than superseded: the old categorial form enters the new as an element within it. "In historical time or causality, all preceding forms of time or causality are present, but they are not the same as they were before."[28]

Tillich's thought has often been criticized as remaining in the Idealistic tradition, as being pre-Darwinian, as not incorporating man in nature as all serious philosophies have had to do since 1859, at the same time that they must emphasize man's distinctive traits and ways of acting. This criticism is justified against much German and French existentialism, though Heidegger himself makes much of the "self-world polarity," and the later Husserl focused on the *Lebenswelt*—man in his environment. Tillich is saved from this charge by his allegiance to the evolutionary emphasis of Schelling. His "philosophy of life" places him in the group of philosophers of "emergent evolution" of the first part of our century along with Lloyd-Morgan, Samuel Alexander, Whitehead, and Dewey and, among the Germans, Nicolai Hartmann.

Tillich is not primarily the prophet, the man whose sincerity and stamp of inspiration bring immediate conviction—save in his remarkable and impressive sermons—but rather the philosopher, whose appeal lies in his mastery of reason and rational argument. Paul Tillich seems to me not only the ablest Protestant theologian of the passing generation, but also by far the most persuasive exponent in English of the philosophy of existentialism and, what is more to the point, a real contributor to the present-day revival of metaphysical inquiry. His is a first-rate philosophical mind.

Whether his technical philosophy will endure as a legacy depends on the future of Existentialism. This is a philosophy that seems difficult for most professional philosophers in England and America to take very seriously at the moment. I suspect that what will endure and enter into subsequent philosophical thought is likely to be some of his great wealth of specific insights, rather than his cherished system of ontology as a whole.

Notes

1. Paul Tillich, *Systematic Theology* (3v). Chicago, 1963. III, 4. Further references to this book give volume and page only.
2. III, 203.
3. I, 7.
4. II, 13.
5. I, 8.
6. II, 13.
7. II, 15.
8. II, 15–16.
9. II, 16.
10. II, 27.
11. For the Ph.D.: *Die religionsgeschichtliche Konstruction in Schellings positiver Philosophie, ihre Voraussetzungen und Prinzipien* (1910); for the Licentiate in Theology: *Mystik und Schuldbewusstsein in Schellings philosophischer Entwicklung* (1912).
12. See "Kairos and Logos," in *Interpretation of History* (written in 1926); and "The Structure of Reason," in *Systematic Theology*, I, 71–88.
13. Cf. "The Two Types of Philosophy of Religion" (1946), in Tillich's *Theology of Culture*.
14. Cf. Tillich, *End of the Protestant Era* (1948), esp. ch. 5, "Realism and Faith" (written 1926).

15. I, 18.
16. I, 22.
17. I, 72.
18. I, 79.
19. I, 80.
20. I, 97.
21. I, 98.
22. I, 99.
23. I, 102.
24. I, 102–3.
25. I, 103.
26. I, 105.
27. III, 25.
28. III, 18.

Paul Tillich
as a Contemporary Theologian

Roger L. Shinn
Union Theological Seminary

To anyone who has known Paul Tillich as a teacher, senior colleague, and warm friend, there is a temptation to turn an analysis of his thought into an act of piety. Happily Tillich shows the way out of the temptation. He was the kind of scholar for whom the fitting act of piety is rigorous encounter with his mind and spirit. Here I shall aim to enter into such encounter.

This occasion calls for a discussion of Tillich's theology as a whole rather than some single segment of it; yet it requires a brief inquiry. In an effort to maintain some sharpness of focus on a remarkably wide-ranging thinker, I have chosen to ask the one question: Is Tillich's theology authentically *contemporary?*

I raise this question, I hope, without any illusion that the contemporary mood is the touchstone of truth and wisdom. It is always possible that a thinker may be the more powerful and helpful because he antagonizes the contemporary mind rather than merging with it. Yet I propose that the question is a legitimate one to bring to Paul Tillich, because he devoted his career to a contemporary reinterpretation of theology.

In this regard Tillich contrasted himself to Karl Barth, whose theology, he charged, "wishes to resurrect the dogmatic doctrines of the Reformation by by-passing the scientific work of the last two hundred years."[1] Although he greatly admired Barth, he could warn sharply against the return of the Grand Inquisitor, "wearing the strong but tight-fitting armor of Barthian supranaturalism."[2] Tillich continuously sought to translate traditional theology into a language meaningful to contemporaries. Then when his own phrases became cliches in the mouths of his admirers, he tried to retranslate again and again. He did so with considerable effectiveness. Theologian Daniel Day Williams has praised "Tillich's extraordinary power to speak to contemporary culture in its own terms."[3] He was a preacher of haunting influence—a rare trait in a theologian so scholarly as he. His spell was so great that he became a legend during his own lifetime. His name appeared on the cover of the *Saturday Evening Post* along with those of two culture-heroes, Ty Cobb and Brigitte Bardot.[4] (Happily he was spared the rivalry that might have arisen if pictures of the three had appeared together.) He won that peculiarly American form of homage represented by a cover portrait on Time. Clearly it seems that he was a man among his contemporaries, a man of his time.

Thus he frequently was called to meet challengers from the theological right, who believed that he betrayed the biblical faith and the Christian theological tradition. Granted, during his first few years in America, following his exile from Germany in 1933, some of his critics accused him of "neo-orthodoxy," even "neo-supranaturalism." Their chief evidence, so far as I can tell, was his German accent. Soon he earned recognition as an innovator in theology who left no traditional doctrine unscrutinized or unchanged. Nels Ferré argued that Tillich's symbols failed to "imply the structural content of historic Christian affirmation"[5] and later went on to charge that "there is no more dangerous theological leader alive."[6] *Life* in an obituary described him as "the great radical theologian" and "apostle to the skeptics."[7]

Tillich's reply to such characterizations, whether pronounced in accusation or in praise, was to insist on the futility of echoing the past and on the necessity of reinterpretation. The modern experience, he insisted, has affinities with human experience in other times, but is not identical with that of any past. Instead of repeating the language of his Lutheran heritage concerning the forgiveness of sin, Tillich developed the theme of one of his most influential books, *The Courage To Be* (New Haven 1952): that modern man's anxiety of "emptiness and meaninglessness" must be distinguished from medieval man's anxiety of "guilt and condemnation" or ancient man's anxiety "of fate and death" —even though the three are not totally separable. While maintaining this position, Tillich insisted that he was nevertheless a faithful interpreter (even if a reinterpreter) of the biblical faith. In his short book, *Biblical Religion and the Search for Ultimate Reality* (Chicago 1955), as in his three-volume *Systematic Theology* (Chicago 1963), he sought to refute charges that he was unbiblical. By his latter years he was well accustomed to handling attacks from the theological right.

The new experience in the autumn of his career was that of meeting theological critics who argued that he was out of date. Tillich's fault, said these men, was not reckless innovation but refusal to become contemporary. Paul van Buren, for example, has endorsed the criticism that Tillich was "a 19th century German idealist, quite unfamiliar with the philosophical climate of the English-speaking world in the 20th century." In the face of "the cultural gap between Tillich's world and our own," says van Buren, Tillich's popularity had to be understood as that of a "fatherly figure" speaking to a nostalgia for a bygone world.[8] Harvey Cox, arguing that religion and metaphysics "are disappearing forever,"[9] pronounces Tillich passé for his ontological inquiries and his attempt to foist on modern man "religious" questions that this man does not really ask. Cox, approving theology but not religion in his secular city, finds Barth more contemporary than Tillich; so he seeks to refute Tillich and to go beyond Barth.[10]

Not all of the "radical theologians" are so condescending toward Tillich. The aging *enfants terribles*, Thomas Altizer and William Hamilton, dedicate their common book "In Memory of Paul Tillich,"[11] and Altizer writes, "Tillich is the modern father of radical theology."[12] This tribute is not convincing to those theologians who regard Altizer and Hamilton as basically nineteenth-century thinkers—Altizer as a Hegelian-style metaphysician and Hamilton as a product of the romantic movement. And, in any case, their praise of Tillich carries an implication that the father has not kept up with the sons. Hence Tillich himself wondered, at least occasionally, whether intellectual history was passing him by. In an unpublished but influential paper, Langdon Gilkey, Tillich's colleague at the University of Chicago, reported a conversation in which Tillich pensively commented on the feeling of becoming out-dated. A few critics have built too much on that interchange. Tillich characteristically expressed himself in many moods, and on other occasions in his last months he showed himself eager to take on all comers in spirited controversy. But the incident shows that the subject of this inquiry is a real one.

The issue arises out of some deeply pervasive strains in Tillich's thought. He was a mystic in a pragmatic culture, a biblical theologian and preacher in a technological age, an existentialist in a functional society, an ontologist and in a way a rationalist in a positivistic era, a philosopher of religion in a time when many theologians as well as secularists scorned both philosophy and religion. Thus he might be described as a marginal man in a society that makes strong demands for conformity—or, to use his own favorite phrase, a man "on the boundary." In such a position a thinker and prophet may be either unusually powerful or irrelevant. Obviously Tillich had some kind of rare power. I shall, therefore, examine the issue of his contemporaneity in regard to three specific questions: (1) Was Tillich right in taking religion seriously? (2) How seriously did he take doubt? (3) Is systematic theology possible today?

Religion

Was Tillich right in taking religion seriously? In current theological vocabulary religion is often something to be held in contempt, and many theologians, European and American, have criticized Tillich for his appreciation of religion.

Obviously some sorting out of meanings is needed here. The theological criticism of religion begins with the Old Testament prophets, who make their biting attacks upon the cultic activities of a wicked people who prefer rituals and sacrifices to justice and mercy. Today orators and editorialists frequently regard religion as immune from criticism—like such other sacred symbols as the affluent society, American foreign policy, and the F.B.I. But the theological tradition has always been less reverent. It has long insisted that religion, judged by a penetrating ethical standard and surely by any ethical insights derived from Jesus Christ, may be good or bad. What is relatively new is the theological judgment that the incarnation has conferred a validity upon everything human *except* religion, which is inherently bad. Since Barth's early attacks upon religion and Dietrich Bonhoeffer's plea for a "religionless Christianity,"[13] theologians have developed a caution—almost a conditioned reflex—against the word religion.

In seeking the reasons that the word is not in vogue, we came upon several. One common reaction against religion is simply a tactical gambit to elevate Christian revelation above religion. The Christian may be spared the hard analysis of the relation of Christianity to the world religions if he declares his disdain for all religions—usually, with an attempt at modesty, including Christianity in the list—then goes on to acknowledge a Christian revelation that is immune to all the flaws and vices of such human activities as religion. Tillich scorned this tactic. He approached all religions with a generous eagerness to understand them and learn from them. He was too critical to claim that he knew a revelation, untouched by fallibility, that demoted all non-Christian religions to a place of uselessness. Here, surely, Tillich is more contemporary than his critics if we take contemporary to mean anything more than faddish.

A second objection is directed against religion as a segment of experience, a department of life, that belongs primarily to ideology in the sense that it either consecrates the interest of its participants or provides a ceremonial escape from the responsibilities of life in society. On this theme Tillich could be as caustic as any of the critics of religion and he matched them at their own language game. As early as 1922 he wrote an essay called "Overcoming the Notion of Religion within the Philosophy of Religion."[14] Twenty years later he wrote, "The first word . . . to be spoken by religion to the people of our time must be a word against religion."[15]

But Tillich preferred a non-polemical definition of religion. "Religion is the state of being grasped by an ultimate concern, a concern which qualifies all other concerns as preliminary and which itself contains the answer to the question of the meaning of our life."[16] Again, "The name for the reception of revelation is 'religion.' "[17] Thus understood, "Religion, like God, is omnipresent; its presence, like that of God, can be forgotten, neglected, denied. But it is always effective, giving inexhaustible depth to life and inexhaustible meaning to every cultural creation."[18] A consequence is that "There is no wall between the religious and the nonreligious."[19] Long before the current theological enthusiasm for the secular, Tillich endorsed a "passion toward the profane" and a "passion for the secular."[20]

Such a conception of religion is immune to most of the common theological attacks, which have another target. But even so, some theologians argue with Tillich. They suspect that Tillich may be trying to put something over on people by denying them the chance to be irreligious. Dietrich Bonhoeffer in his prison letter wrote, "Tillich set out to interpret the evolution of the world itself—against its will—in a religious sense, to give it its whole shape through religion. That was very courageous of him, but the world unseated him and went on by itself: he too sought to understand the world better than it understood itself, but it felt entirely *mis*understood, and rejected the imputation."[21]

In Bonhoeffer's argument there is an implication that the theologian might better recognize and applaud a healthy secularity in the world than seek for some hidden cravings or mystical intuitions. Maybe man is not naturally religious, now that the world has come "of age," and there is something cheap in trying to cultivate religious experience. Above all Bonhoeffer rejects the technique of theologians who seek to batter man into an existentialist despair, to come flying to his rescue with their doctrine of salvation.

Harvey Cox, aiming to build on Bonhoeffer, says that Tillich's religious questions "do not occur to the newly emergent urban-secular man." Pragmatic man does not need to ask Tillich's "ultimate" and "existential" questions, says Cox.[22] The anxieties and the consequent need for courage, as described by the existentialists, are simply unreal. However, Cox is not consistent. Later he writes, "It is his experience of the transcendent which makes man man."[23] And as he describes this experience it is remarkably akin to Tillich's description of religion.[24]

Is there, then, a real issue here? Probably there is, although not nearly so clear-cut as Tillich's challengers assume. Paul Tillich was himself a man of extraordinary aesthetic, ontological, "religious," and mystic sensitivity. By his own testimony he "wrestled with the idea of the Infinite" at the age of eight.[25] He explored the inner meanings of anxiety both in their immediate impact and as interpreted through existentialism and psychotherapy. The critic may ask whether he was cultivating esoteric experiences as an apologetic technique. Or was he unearthing the experiences that more ordinary people keep buried? Bonhoeffer's writings, like his poem, "Who am I?"[26] seem to say the second.

Tillich's own answer is clear. If contemporary man is not religious, it is because he has lost the "dimension of depth." "He has lost the courage to ask such questions with an infinite seriousness—as former generations did—and he has lost the courage to receive answers to these questions, wherever they may come from."[27] To reverse Gilbert Murray's figure of speech, superficiality, not depth, is the failure of nerve. Man *is* religious—often in terribly cheapened and distorted ways, but inherently religious. If contemporary society, dominated by technical reason and bourgeois institutions, has become religiously insensitive, that is the failure of courage in the society, not its strength.

Doubt and Faith

How seriously did Tillich take doubt? At first glance the question may seem unnecessary. Has anybody since Soren Kierkegaard described more realistically and sympathetically the interpenetration of faith and doubt? Has anybody exposed more surely the dogmatisms and heteronomous authorities that conceal doubt? For Tillich there can be no faith that does not incorporate, even welcome, doubt into itself. Thus he wrote:

> If faith is understood as being ultimately concerned, doubt is a necessary element in it. . . . Faith includes courage. Therefore, it can include the doubt about itself. . . . Existential doubt and faith are poles of the same reality, the state of ultimate concern.[28]

Thus Tillich took doubt more seriously than most theologians have done. He never suppressed it or brushed it off as trivial; on the contrary he kept digging into human experience to discover the doubt that many believers deny is there.

Early in his career Tillich encountered piercing doubt. As a chaplain in the German army at the Battle of Champagne in 1915, he spent a night among the wounded and dying soldiers, an experience that was shattering to his intellectualist philosophy. Then, as he recounts it:

> I well remember sitting in the woods in France reading Nietzsche's *Thus Spake Zarathustra,* as many other German soldiers did, in a continuous state of exaltation. This was the final liberation from heteronomy. European nihilism carried

Nietzsche's prophetic word that 'God is dead.' Well, the traditional concept of God was dead.[29]

The significance of such a record is to show that Tillich built his theology *after* the encounter with the Nietzschean polemic and with the nihilism that followed Nietzsche. The skeptical challenge to faith was the presupposition of his theology, not an afterthought. Here his history differs from that of many of the next generation of theologians, who developed their thinking along the lines of a rather dogmatic neo-orthodoxy then at mid-career encountered Nietzsche and the criticisms that shook their systems. Tillich's "shaking of the foundations" came early and he developed his theology not to be immune to tremors but to include them within his belief.

Thus Tillich unquestionably took doubt seriously. Yet we must still ask, "In the very *last* analysis how seriously did he take it?" Phenomenologically, he recognized it. Existentially, he acknowledged it. But in *one* sense the inner drive of his thinking may have led to a victory that was more of form than of substance.

Let us start with a single statement of Tillich, momentarily taken out of context. "There is no possible atheism."[30] What does this mean? Certainly Tillich does not mean to deny a widespread phenomenon called atheism. But he does deny its reality in a double sense.

His first response to atheism is that the atheist, too, has his faith, his religion, his ultimate concern. Even as he verbalizes his denials he makes his affirmations. Here, I propose, is a thesis worth examining. The atheist may respond by denying Tillich's case and by resenting Tillich's claim to understand him better than he understands himself. But here the atheist may or may not be right. If a man tells a psychiatrist, "I have no anxieties or frustrations," the psychiatrist does not immediately accept the testimony as self-authenticating. Similarly, if a man tells a theologian, "I have no religion, or I am an atheist," the theologian need not simply agree without further conversation. The Tillichian theologian will want to inquire into the man's experiences. If the man is an artist or writer, the theologian will examine his creative works to see whether he finds signs there of what theology calls belief. Frequently Tillich can show cogently that the professed atheist actually shows something much like Tillich's definition of religion. All this is a legitimate form of inquiry, provided the theologian looks for the evidence that is really there and does not impose his own experience or idea upon somebody else. Such a process may possibly lead to the conclusion that there are no atheists. But any such pronouncement is clearly *a posteriori*, depending upon the reading of the evidence. As such, it remains debatable. My own judgment is that Tillich often reads the evidence with great insight and argues persuasively with those who read it differently. At this point Tillich's thesis is understandable and discussable, and it may indeed be true.

But the second side of Tillich's thesis is a little different. Here he moves into what sometimes appears to be an *a priori* denial of the possibility of radical doubt and unbelief. The clearest exposition of this thesis comes in his book, *Dynamics of Faith*, where he describes both the "subjective" and the "objective" meaning of faith.[31] Tillich here first defines faith as "the state of being ultimately concerned."[32] This definition leads to a humanistic, anthropological description of faith. The second definition is that faith is "the concern about the unconditional," "the passion for the infinite."[33] This leads to a theological and ontological description of the God, who, because of his unconditional and ultimate character, can alone be the source of faith.

At this stage of the analysis comes the crucial declaration. "The ultimate of the act of faith and the ultimate that is meant in the act of faith are one and the same."[34] That is, to Tillich it is inconceivable that man's ultimate concern not be directed toward ultimate being or that ultimate being should not grasp and claim man's ultimate response. But perhaps exactly this is the debatable point.

The thesis of *Dynamics of Faith* is stated earlier and more elaborately in Volume I of the *Systematic Theology*. Here Tillich writes: "God . . . is the name for that which concerns man ultimately."[35] He makes a thoughtful and persuasive analysis of the relation of preliminary and ultimate concerns. Then he moves from the existential to the ontological statement. He knows well that men in their illusions and idolatries may seem to find their strongest concerns in illusions or parochial causes. But in the last analysis, he insists:

> That which concerns us ultimately must belong to reality as a whole; it must belong to being. Otherwise we could not encounter it and it could not concern us. Of course, it cannot be one being among others; then it would not concern us infinitely. It must be the ground of our being, that which determines our being or not-being, the ultimate unconditional power of being.[36]

I do not want to argue against Tillich's conclusion. I find it persuasive. My own opinion is that all Christian theology, in one way or another, agrees with Tillich's thesis or something close to it. What I am maintaining is that the thesis is discussable, not self-evident. If an atheist wishes to argue that man's deepest concerns have no grounding in reality outside himself, or that in this universe power and morality are ultimately unrelated to each other, I do not think we can exclude the argument from serious discourse. Tillich almost excludes it by definition—i.e., by defining ultimate concern as concern directed toward being itself. But, as he knows well in his criticism of the ontological argument for the existence of God, no case can be won by definition.

So it is in this sense and this sense only that I wonder whether Tillich has finally failed to take doubt seriously and has thereby met obliquely rather than directly one aspect of the contemporary mind. When I say this I must immediately add or repeat that he had met the conventional doubts more seriously than most of the doubters themselves. When Tillich affirms faith in God as against atheism he has already removed from his concept of God a nest of superstitions that most people are unprepared to give up. On many a skirmish Tillich is closer to conventional skepticism than to conventional belief, and his affirmations give little comfort to that curious mixture of Christian piety and the American way of life that no one can attack without risking charges of blasphemy. Tillich's doubts are more radical than most of our culture is able to comprehend. I am not asking whether he should have been more radical, but whether he should have taken more seriously a type of doubt different from his own.

Systematic Theology

Is systematic theology possible today? Perhaps, as Kierkegaard believed, systematic theology is never possible. But we had better start from the more modest judgment that this is not an age of the unified vision and of system building in the tradition of Plato, Aristotle, Spinoza, and Hegel—or of Origen, St. Thomas Aquinas, and John Calvin. The major inquiries of our time are more fragmentary. Men seek to make decisions, resolve problems, accept whatever illumination they can find on the human condition, derive a few truths about experience that can be framed in one or another of several "language games" that never get fully integrated with each other.

For a while, of course, the logical positivists tried to whittle down the scope of philosophy, eliminating metaphysics, ethics, and theology from the domain of meaningful inquiry. By this time it has become rather obvious that most of those positivists were themselves thinly disguised metaphysicians, moralists, and priests. Tillich plainly was not a positivist.

But system building is questioned by more than the positivists. Any thinker recognizes that all his fragmentary insights have wider meanings, that he must check these out and strive for consistency. But today most theologians and philosophers do this in a rather tentative way. They find gaps and apparent conflicts in their apprehensions. They would like to overcome these, but when they cannot, they take comfort in the advice of Whitehead who, even though he was a system builder, said that a clash of detail "should not lead us hastily to abandon doctrines for which we have solid evidence."[37] In such a situation metaphysical adventures are likely to be modest and spare, and theology is likely to be pluralistic—certainly in its apprehension of society, but also in its own formulations and perhaps even its sense of reality.

In this setting Paul Tillich deliberately entitled his major work *Systematic Theology* and defended the responsibility of the theologian to think systematically. When in 1956 the Jesuit, Gustave Weigel, found too much existentialism in Tillich's theology, Tillich replied: "With respect to my ontological thought generally, I want to state that it is much less influenced by existentialism than by Aristotle and Schelling."[38] No one was surprised by the reference to Schelling, but some—I was one—did not expect the mention of Aristotle. Yet it was a valid reminder of Tillich's respect for the philosophical-ontological tradition and of his high regard for the capacity of reason.

Skeptics may wonder whether theology ever meets the demands of reason. Julius Penrose, in a novel by James Gould Cozzens, says, "If hypocrisy can be said to be the homage vice pays to virtue, theology could be said to be a homage nonsense tries to pay to sense."[39] Cozzens scores a point against any theology that accepts an arbitrary authority, then uses its rational ingenuity to support the authoritative deliverances or work out their implications. This was not Tillich's method. In one sense, it is true, he was not a rationalist. God, he wrote, "cannot be approached in any other way than through an act of faith."[40] But this faith is not irrational; it is very close to "ecstatic reason" or "reason in the state of ultimate concern."[41] Tillich's thought was about as free from superstitious irrationalities as any man's can be. Certainly he was open to all the evidence that scientific reason might offer on any subject. We cannot imagine Tillich becoming disturbed if scientists should find evidence of life on other planets or change its estimates of the age of the earth or the processes of evolution.

But Tillich was more interested in "ontological reason" than in "technical reason." Ontological reason "enables the mind to grasp and to transform reality."[42] Here man does not simply think *about* the world, himself, and the processes of being. He participates in these.

On this issue Tillich comes from the tradition of philosophical idealism with its long heritage tracing back to Plato. He could, in fact, write: "I am epistemologically an idealist, if idealism means the assertion of the identity of thought and being as the principle of truth."[43] Inevitably the question arises: does Tillich's drive toward an ontological system lead him to overemphasize unity and coherence, moving him in the direction of monism and pantheism?

Unquestionably such a thrust is at work within his thinking. But it meets certain counter-thrusts. The first of these is the German romanticism that infused so much *Sturm und Drang* into Tillich. "Classical composure and harmony were not part of my heritage," he wrote.[44] Second, he felt the power of Kierkegaard, who "was the first to break through the closed system of the idealist philosophy of essence."[45] Third, Karl Marx refuted for him the idealistic rationalism by exposing the ideological nature of thought. From Kierkegaard and Marx he learned "that the highest possibility for achieving non-ideological truth is given at the point of profoundest meaninglessness, through the deepest despair, in man's greatest estrangement from his own nature."[46] Such a statement moves far out of the orbit of monistic idealism.

One rather different influence deserves mention: his movement to America. Of this he could say, "The interdependence of theory and practice in Anglo-Saxon culture, religious as well as secular, has freed me from the fascination of that kind of abstract idealism which enjoys the system for the system's sake."[47]

The man who could write that was not guilty of the arid abstractions that have often plagued systems. When all is said and done, Tillich had a profound recognition of the dynamic and pluralistic character of life and all being. God, he said, "is the eternal process in which separation is posited and is overcome by reunion."[48] That idea may not be congenial to every workaday empiricism, but surely there is nothing staid or static in it. System had not overcome vitality. Yet he was uneasy with the idea of "God as becoming." And occasionally he returned to one of the most ancient of philosophers whom he especially loved, Parmenides, and to the doctrine that "being is older than becoming." Such a doctrine *might* lead to the triumph of unity and system over movement and life.

Was Tillich's effort as a system, then, a mistake? Is systematic theology really impossible? In considering such a question, it is hard to bring a criticism against Tillich that he has not anticipated and stated even more strongly than his critics. Let me state my own judgment in an unabashedly personal way, then give his answer.

During the last months of Tillich's life I had the opportunity to write a review of the baker's dozen of his books that had appeared in paperback reprints. I raised the question I had often asked about his system: "Can he really bring off the attempt or is his synthesis a precarious one that must shatter as soon as it is separated from his personal magic?"

My tentative answer was to say, "If Tillich can achieve his aim he is one of the thinkers of the ages. Even if he cannot he has made a heroic effort. Perhaps he will be remembered, not for the achievement of his impressive system, but for his more modest aim, expressed in *The Protestant Era* . . . to anticipate 'a new form of Christianity, to be expected and prepared for, but not yet to be named.' "[49]

Those remarks were printed in the *New York Times Book Review* dated September 19, 1965. Because of a strike they were actually distributed with the Sunday *Times* of October 17, 1965. Five days later, on October 22, Tillich died. I do not know whether he saw my comment. In a way it does not matter. We had talked about the issue before. And although I was eager for his reply, I did not need it. He has already given it in defining "the Protestant principle" of "the divine and human protest against any absolute claim made for a relative reality."[50] Nobody had to remind Tillich to apply that principle to his own work as to everything else.

I have examined the contemporaneity of Paul Tillich in three major aspects of his thinking. I can best conclude by returning to one of his favorite themes. He was a man "on the boundary" in an age of specialists and people seeking secure homes. So he said of himself, "At almost every point, I have had to stand between alternative possibilities of existence, to be completely at home in neither and to take no definite stand against either."[51] He recalled Abraham, commanded by God, "Go from your home . . . to the land that I will show you." And of Abraham he said:

> He is bidden to leave his native soil, the community of his family and cult, his people and state, for the sake of a promise that he does not understand. The God who demands obedience of him is the God of an alien country, a God of history, who means to bless all the races of the earth.[52]

Living on the boundary, Tillich was too modern, too venturesome, for the orthodox. Yet he was not sufficiently at home for those exultant in the freedom of the secular city.

His vocation on the boundary may be the reason that he is not quite the man for this—or any—season. The same reason may make him, in a more meaningful sense, a man for all seasons.

Notes

1. Paul Tillich, *On the Boundary: An Autobiographical Sketch* (New York: Scribners, 1966), p. 49.
2. *Ibid.*, p. 41.
3. Daniel Day Williams, review of Tillich, *Systematic Theology*, Vol. I, *The Christian Century*, August 1, 1951.
4. *Saturday Evening Post*, June 14, 1958.
5. Nels F. S. Ferré, "Tillich's View of the Church," in *The Theology of Paul Tillich*, ed. by Charles W. Kegley and Robert W. Bretall (New York: Macmillan, 1952), p. 250.
6. Ferré, review of Tillich, *The New Being*, Interpretation IX:465–67 (October, 1955).
7. *Life*, November 5, 1965.
8. Paul van Buren, review of Tillich, *Systematic Theology*, Vol. III, *Christian Century*, February 5, 1964, p. 178.
9. Harvey Cox, *The Secular City* (New York: Macmillan, 1965), p. 4.
10. *Ibid.*, pp. 78–83. Cox's publisher evidently missed the point, because the cover of the book classifies it under "religion." And Cox, when he sees "ontology" disappear in Barth, misses the highly speculative trend that emerged in Barth's *Church Dogmatics*.
11. Thomas J. J. Altizer and William Hamilton, *Radical Theology*

and the Death of God (Indianapolis, New York, and Kansas City: Bobbs Merrill, 1966).

12. Altizer, *The Gospel of Christian Atheism* (Philadelphia: Westminster, 1966), p. 10.

13. Dietrich Bonhoeffer, *Prisoner for God: Letters and Papers from Prison* (New York: Macmillan, 1955), passim.

14. See bibliography in *The Theology of Paul Tillich*, p. 354. The essay is described briefly in Tillich, *The Protestant Era* (Chicago: University of Chicago Press, 1948), p. xvi.

15. *The Protestant Era*, p. 185.

16. Paul Tillich, *Christianity and the Encounter of the World Religions* (New York: Columbia University Press, 1964), p. 4.

17. Paul Tillich, *Biblical Religion and the Search for Ultimate Reality* (Chicago: University of Chicago Press, 1955), p. 3.

18. *The Protestant Era*, pp. xv–xvi.

19. *Ibid.*, p. xv.

20. *On the Boundary*, pp. 71, 73.

21. *Prisoner for God*, pp. 147–48, entry of June 8, 1944.

22. *The Secular City*, p. 79.

23. *Ibid.*, p. 261.

24. *Ibid.*, p. 262. "Thus we meet God at those places in life where we come up against that which is not pliable and disposable, at those hard edges where we are both stopped and challenged to move ahead. God meets us as the transcendent, as those aspects of our experience which can never be transmuted into extensions of ourselves." The similarity between Tillich's boundaries and Cox's edges is instructive.

25. *On the Boundary*, p. 30.

26. *Prisoner for God*, p. 165.

27. Paul Tillich, "The Lost Dimension in Religion," *Saturday Evening Post*, June 14, 1958.

28. Paul Tillich, *Dynamics of Faith* (New York: Harper and Row, 1957), pp. 18, 20, 22. The same theme is developed in the famous discussion of "the God above God." See *The Courage to Be* (New Haven: Yale University Press, 1952), pp. 186–90.

29. Reported in Time, March 16, 1959, p. 7. The source is apparently an interview. Tillich refers indirectly to the experience in *On the Boundary* (p. 53), and his writings include frequent allusions to Nietzsche.

30. *The Protestant Era*, p. xv.
31. *Dynamics of Faith*, p. 9.
32. *Ibid.*, p. 1.
33. *Ibid.*, p. 9.
34. *Ibid.*, p. 11.
35. Paul Tillich, *Systematic Theology*, Volume I (Chicago: University of Chicago Press, 1951), p. 211.
36. *Ibid.*, p. 21.
37. Alfred North Whitehead, *Science and the Modern World* (New York: New American Library, Mentor Book, 1948), p. 184.
38. *Gregorianum*, XXXVII (1956), 1, p. 54.
39. James Gould Cozzens, *By Love Possessed* (Greenwich, Connecticut: Fawcett, 1959), p. 216.
40. *Dynamics of Faith*, pp. 10–11.
41. *Ibid.*, p. 76. "Faith is the act in which reason reaches ecstatically beyond itself."
42. *Systematic Theology*, Vol. I, p. 72. Cf. *Dynamics of Faith*, p. 75.
43. *On the Boundary*, p. 82.
44. *Ibid.*, p. 15.
45. *Ibid.*, p. 84.
46. *Ibid.*, p. 86.
47. *The Protestant Era*, p. x.
48. *Systematic Theology*, Vol. I, p. 242.
49. *New York Times Book Review*, September 19, 1965. The quotation from Tillich is from the preface to *The Protestant Era*, p. xxii.
50. *The Protestant Era*, p. 163.
51. *On the Boundary*, p. 13.
52. *Ibid.*, p. 91.

The Psychiatric Legacy of Paul Tillich

Earl A. Loomis, Jr., M.D.
Attending Psychiatrist
St. Luke's Hospital, New York

I

*F*ew clergymen and fewer theologians had time for the light from Vienna which seemed to be focused disconcertingly on the skeletons in the closet of Everyman. Freud's essays and remarks about the religions of the past and of his time were met with general defensiveness. To be sure, in Zurich there was Pastor Oskar Pfister.[1] Although surrounded in his home city by members of Jung's secession, he was an early and faithful supporter of Freud. Within the theological world, his was a lonely voice. Himself a psychoanalyst, he bent much of his efforts toward clinical rather than philosophical emphases. Psychoanalysis began and continued for a long time as an identified enemy of religion, despite its stalwart defense by this loyal protagonist.

In time the pioneers in pastoral care, pastoral counseling and modern religious education became curious about psychoanalysis in a positive sense, adapting and applying psychoanalytic theory and practice to religious concerns. But often the enthusiasm of their followers was greater than theoretical grasp or validity of the application. It became easy to get on or off the bandwagon, and multitudes did.

As early as 1919–1921, during the aftermath of World War I (in which he had served as a field chaplain with the German Army), Tillich was familiar with the theories of psychoanalysis that had penetrated into European intellectual minds. Intellectual acquaintanceship with psychoanalysis may perhaps constitute a worthy prelude; often it serves as a substitute for emotional or existential insight. For Tillich at that time analysis remained somewhat of an enigma at a personal or depth level.

As late as 1933 to 1937, in facing his disillusionment with fatherland and German culture, he was groping for the place of psychoanalysis in his philosophical system, and for him it still remained somewhat isolated and peripheral. His recovery of the idea of the "demonic" doubtless served him as one major bridge between religio-philosophical and analytic thinking. His circle of "bohemian" socio-political friends put him constantly in touch with analytically informed intellectuals. Rilke's poetry with its overtones of depth psychology was an esthetic bridge.[2] Nevertheless the effort to assimilate and accomodate himself to psychoanalysis was a difficult one for Tillich, as for many others of his time. Persisting, his curiosity eventually was rewarded and the interchange that grew out of his close alliance with analysis and analytic thought was enduring.

In time he came to speak and write as one who had seen the problems and the conflicts, one who had experienced the drives and the defenses, one who had struggled with the resistances and the transference. Eventually the familiarity became deep and lasting. Tillich's capacity to manifest comprehension and empathy in talking with analysts endeared him to them and among many of their number he had close friends and lasting admirers. To say that he ministered to them would be almost an understatement; to say that he lectured to them would be an overstatement. Often he listened more than he talked, but when he preached he was listened to by analysts of any or no religion.

As a man Tillich revealed a quality of openness to other men of diverse backgrounds and interests. As a philosopher his openness was a capacity for integrating and synthesizing that which seemed superficially divergent. *Superficial* similarity did not, however, interest Tillich. He focused rather upon deeper linkages and correlations. Intimations of profound and basic relatedness challenged him to explore ways to integrate that which *seemed* different and ways to distinguish that which seemed similar. Bending every effort to avoid confusing orders of knowledge, he repeatedly insisted upon demonstrating valid continuities, parallels, and polarities between the observed facts and our ways of theorizing or fitting them into meaningful systematic wholes.

Tillich's method did not subsume the physical beneath the emotional, the emotional beneath the mental. Rather it viewed the whole of man's life and world as interwoven in terms of dimensions rather than levels. Dimensions can be interpenetrating and can reflect various degrees of continuity and discontinuity. *Levels,* on the contrary, are less adaptable to the orders of truth. They also tend to introduce the implication of priority or of superior *versus* inferior value. But each *dimension* has its own unique meaning and value for understanding a human being as a unified but multidimensional person.

In asserting the importance of his method of correlation Tillich affirms that knowledge in no single dimension can be complete or exclusive of others. Furthermore he asserts that—try as we will—we cannot approach the interpretation of a body of facts, let alone collect or educe them, without an underlying point of view. Whether he knows it or not (of course it is better to know!) each worker's metaphysical foundations are not only present but also active and influential in where and how he seeks facts, selects data, and derives conclusions. Sir William Osler said, in effect, that to practice medicine without theory is to sail an uncharted sea;

to theorize without practicing is never to go to sea at all. The charts make a better explorer and the explorations correct and improve the charts. Tillich's theory of cognition maintains that there is a resonance and a relevance between the questions the facts pose for us and the way our minds go about arriving at conclusions. The inner method and its underlying principles constitute a latent metaphysics in each of us. As metaphysician Tillich seemed to draw upon a vast reservoir of answers. And the meaning he sought from each was only to become clear as, one by one, the relevant questions could be posed. Of course his answers were questing ones and hence were latent questions, even as the questions he sought were answers as well. Once the correlations were begun the linkages themselves evoked in turn a clarification or reorganization of additional answers, ready themselves for correlation with new questions. This done, the earlier correlations were constantly subject to higher, deeper or broader orders of questions. The fact that a theologian of Tillich's stature and a philosopher of his erudition saw in psychiatry and psychoanalysis a rich source of provocative and relevant questions is alone of sufficient importance to justify our sense of indebtedness to him. His approach should give pause to those who deem metaphysics to be too far removed from the real world or who would imagine that their own data have no bearing on philosophy. In the words of William Cole, ". . . the facts of life must always be related to the meaning of life. The two elements can never be entirely separated, so that the facts cannot be left to science and their interpretation to religion."[3]

Having adduced such correspondences one should certainly not presume to use one set of relations, propositions or data to prove the truth of another in a different dimension. Rather the linkage might serve to illustrate the utility of exposing our formulations for each level to their opposite numbers for another. Such applications have demonstrated their fruitfulness in numerous fields of research and practice and our affinity for "trying them on for size" suggests that many of us share the underlying assumption that the physical universe and its biological inhabitants can be seen as corresponding to the structures of our thought. Whether this is a tautology, an apriorism or a testable postulate is a moot point. Without some such assumption, however, I wonder if any researcher would have any idea of what and where to seek or what to do with what he found. The implications for epistemology seem to be clear: gaps in an otherwise symmetrical matrix—as for example the Periodic Table—serve as invitation and impetus to seek the missing elements. The capacity of the mind to create an organized pattern into which observed data fit requires the further capacity to conceive the unknown, to postulate a matrix of possibilities, to seek the missing links, to achieve closure, to test and correct the design for commensurability with the evidence, and ultimately to approach validation that is simultaneously empirical and logical.

Almost every one of Tillich's theological concerns has direct bearing on psychiatry. I can illustrate with only one or two examples. The first is the polarity of separation and union, the relation of individuality to participation. This derives from Tillich's philosophical anthropology, a theory that contains a number of elements which are parallel to psychoanalysis and child development.

II

Among other criteria for being a person or a self versus an automaton or something subhuman, one must, according to Tillich, be individual, separate, discrete; but one must also and simultaneously be a participant, engaged and involved in the lives of others. If the polarity is pushed too far in either direction so that one side or the other is inadequately represented, a man ceases to be or become a man. Rather he abdicates his personhood in the isolation and alienation of excessive separateness—or conversely he merges with another being or mass of beings. In Tillich's words, he loses the "courage to be" whether on the one hand as a separate self or on the other hand as a participant. The exclusion of either aspect of selfhood is incompatible with fully developed humanity.

The foregoing formulation corresponds to that of psychoanalytic theory of human development. Individuation is a crucial stage in maturation. The latter has come to recognize that in the course of individuation and socialization of the personality a human being cannot function as a person unless he has come to the point that he can concurrently be both a separate and related self. This means that he must be neither alienated from nor fused with another, must be neither an *isolate* nor a "Siamese twin."

In child psychiatry we have come to use two terms which approximate the meaning of each extreme of the polarity. These are "autism" and "symbiosis." The first describes the developmental phase in which the infant does not or cannot yet form and sustain interhuman relations, but "defines himself" by withdrawing into splendid or horrific isolation. Like the armoured medieval knight he can observe from a distance but he cannot touch or be touched by the object or subject of his interest. By contrast the organism in a symbiotic phase is unable to relate himself to another being, but for a different reason. He is so merged with his symbiotic partner that the absence of differentiation precludes the possibility of coming together or apart. Siamese twins can say neither hello nor goodbye. A pathological symbiotic mother-child relation is one in which each partner of the pair knows the other's thoughts and actions so well that dialogue is superfluous and each can "speak" for the other as well as for himself. Such an infant is therefore undermined in his capacity for transactions.

Children have forces within them and, in normal or average environments, forces without that help them move through their developmental stages to a resolution of each as an exclusive mode and to an adequate balance of both. Hence in most children the normal symbiotic mode is adopted to a reasonable degree and for a reasonable period of time. Becoming a real person means developing the capacity to derive strength for one's individuality from the opposite pole of relatedness. Eventually it means discovering the power to be in relatedness by virtue of one's uniqueness as a separate self. This observation, much oversimplified, which is corroborated by both pathological and normal developmental findings (e.g. Kanner, Spitz, Mahler, et al.) poses a question to Tillich which correlates with his answers in the metaphysical dimension, answers that involve the nature of man and that can be linked with the religious symbols of creation, fall, reconciliation and even the Trinity.

In relating his approach and that of psychoanalysis Tillich is more at home with cross-sectional than with longitudinal formulations of human life. In others words, the historico-genetic approach seems less congenial to his thought forms than does the dynamic-structural method of formulation. Tillich (like Lewin) tends less readily to study process, development, and change than to study conflict, structures, defenses, and the interplay of forces. This tendency is consistent with his approach to history as recognized by Mircea Eliade in the following statement:

> Paul Tillich would never have become a historian of religions, nor, as a matter of fact, a historian of anything else. He was interested in the existential meaning of history— *Geschichte*, not *Historie*. When confronted with archaic, traditional, and oriental religions, he was interested in their historical concreteness and immediacy, not in their modifications or changes or in the results of the flowing of time. He did not deny the importance of the temporal flux for understanding of specific religious forms—but he was primarily interested in their structures; he deciphered their meaning in grasping their structures.[4]

Hence, to my knowledge, the correlation with psychoanalysis was never fully developed by Tillich and never fully worked into his system. The dimension of growth and development seemed unfortunately to have been by-passed and the genetic-historical sequences (both of phylogeny and of ontogeny) consequently received short shrift or were taken for granted.

However, in the light of Tillich's interest in the historical process, I should like to believe that he would have undertaken this further task in years that were, unfortunately, not his to use. Hopefully his successors will fill the breach and develop this aspect of an area which is so crucial for both theory and practice in developmental psychoanalysis. The longitudinal dimension is as indispensable for the history of the individual as for the history of thought.[5] Only in the context of the healing process does Tillich seem to move beyond this limitation. In the latter connection he can think more or less in terms of stages in the process of treatment (and by inference he thereby recognizes their correlation with the incomplete or discordant phases of past development which are in the process of therapeutic decontamination and integration).

The courage to be as a separate self versus the courage to be as a participant—each equally necessary to fulfill and balance the other—is Tillich's parallel to the autistic and symbiotic aspects of the self. Tillich's concept of courage as the power-to-be-in-spite-of-anxiety leads into our next representative parallel: Tillich's concept of anxiety.

III

In a climate in which the sale of tranquilizing medicaments testifies to the prevalence of anxiety and the widespread efforts to be relieved of it, one wonders whether we are dealing with a justifiable reaction to a world suffering from a universal disease, or with a general decline of courage. Tillich says there are two kinds of anxiety: neurotic and existential. Neurotic anxiety can be relieved through psychoanalysis and psychotheraphy. Existential anxiety is inescapable; we must live with it whether we accept or evade it. But the man who evades it is less than alive; he is attenuated, less than a person. The man who accepts it, takes it into himself and acts in spite of it, is the man who exercises what Tillich has called "the courage to be."

An ineradicable core of existential anxiety is man's inevitable position within the conditions of human existence: he is finite, limited, uneasy about the unknown and as yet unknowable; he cannot be certain of the motives, means or consequences of his actions, the limits of his accountability and responsibility, the wholeheartedness of his efforts, the singlemindedness of his endeavors, the clarity of his grasp, the sharpness of his focus, the worthiness of his choices, the validity of his hierarchy of values, comprehensiveness of his scope, and even the meaningfulness (or relevance) of the questions he poses and the answers he seeks.

And yet, without his uneasiness, without this questing, without this seeking for a certainty that does not come, man would be less than man. His very hunger to explain and justify himself, to account for himself, makes every man a sort of philosopher, makes this questing quality in man important to professional philosophers, theologians, and psychotherapists.

For a long time Tillich's notion of existential anxiety puzzled me. It violated my therapeutic frame of reference that a theologian-philosopher should posit a symptom that by definition we could not hope to alleviate. It seemed arbitrary and aprioristic. Are there not happy, uncomplicated people? Are there not the *once born* as well as the *twice born*, to use James's terms? Are we obliged to acknowledge existential anxiety in all times and places and persons wherever and whenever man is designated as man? To be sure Tillich spoke of an Edenic *before* and an eschatological *after* within whose domains man's self-alienation had not yet come to be or had already ceased to be. But these exceptions were expressed in mythical, symbolic forms, and not in a concrete, historical context.

Not only did Tillich seem to have added a needless concept to our already cluttered set of notions about man, he seemed to have neglected normal everyday anxiety as defined and explained in Freud's definitive work on the subject.[6] It is in this work that Freud's earlier conceptions of anxiety are clarified, broadened and focussed into a more general explanatory concept. Up to that point (in analytic circles at least) anxiety had been thought of primarily in two ways: as repeating the birth trauma, or as representing an overflow of indischargable energy—generally as the consequence of frustration—through inhibition imposed from within or without. But now as Freud sharpened his conception of the ego, he could envisage anxiety as a mode of communication within the self, a sign of vigilance, an alarm signal, a warning, a sample of possible pain—but a sample that would, if heeded, help to protect the whole person from harm. Viewed in this way anxiety could be construed as useful, necessary, and serving a survival function. It is like the alarm clock that wakes us. We may curse it for reminding us of our duties of the day, but we would curse it more roundly should it permit us to oversleep! Hence normal anxiety can be appreciated as part of our necessary ego equipment. On the other hand its absence in the face of danger, its presence in times of safety, or its disproportion to the magnitude of threat characterize its pathological varieties, neurotic or psychotic anxiety.

The principal dangers to a human self are threats to its own comfort and integrity and threats to its valued objects in the outside world. To avert danger, vigilance is mandatory. Depending on the ego's capacity for discrimination, anxiety can function as true warning or false alarm concerning the impending loss by and hence impoverishment of the self. If the danger is genuine and if the loss takes place, the result is grief or mourning. As early as 1917 in his *Mourning and Melancholia*, Freud indicated that a man can mourn the loss of a love object (in the sense of a loved person's dying, departing or ceasing to love him); he may also mourn the loss of a part of himself (a limb, function or capacity); he may also mourn the loss of something meaningful and valuable to himself; his nation, his culture or the undermining of that which he has idealized. According to psychoanalytic libido theory these varieties of loss are explicable on the grounds that man can mourn the loss of other than concrete persons, since in any such losses there is an interruption of the bonds of "cathexis," the ties of energy and feeling with which we bind ourselves to that which we love and cherish. If mourning can follow such a loss, why then cannot anxiety herald the *threatened* loss of that which is cathected by the ego, that which is prized by the self? Hence anxiety may be the forewarning of potential grief.

Tillich was able up to a point to accept Freud's anxiety theory; but he never seemed to find it congruent with the libido theory upon which it was based. He preferred to attentuate its continuity with the rest of analytic thought. Again his metaphysical orientation seems to blur and outweigh the biogenetic focus. Whether or not this issue, which may have been largely semantic, was ever resolved for Tillich, I cannot say. Nevertheless he himself has left abundant examples of his willingness to exercise an eagerness for synthesizing his views with those of others. (Perhaps he would forgive my effort to do the same with his own thought.)

I should like to propose that what Tillich called existential anxiety is the normal anxiety of everyday life, the usual signal anxiety, the normal inquietude of human beings in the face of their innate sensitivity to vulnerability. This then would fit within Freud's notion of the unhappiness of everyday life which he feels analysis can never cure,[7] and the cultural discontents which for him are man's lot.[8] Freud even has a mythical parallel to the fall in the primal horde[9] and of the eschatological fulfillment in a world beyond the need for religion.[10]

What then of the ego that allegedly experiences no anxiety? As Tillich, analysts as well are highly dubious. Such a person is deceiving the observer, perhaps himself. If the latter, his anxiety must be expressed in equivalent or substitute manifestations. Some of these substitutions or compensations may appear to him and to the observer as boredom, brashness, indifference, a blasé manner. He may be frenetic or deliberate, carefree or meticulous. But the hallmark of the spurious character of such defences is that when they are sufficiently challenged or blocked, anxiety inevitably emerges. In other words as long as his substitutes go undiscovered and his environment complies, such a person feels and appears totally free of anxiety. But this freedom from discomfort is achieved at a price. The cost is the loss of a part of the self. The more a man isolates himself from his potential for feeling his own and others' pain the less he possesses a broad range or capacity for feeling anything—including pleasure. Whether "felt" or not, anxiety, however, in the long run is a single, unitary phenomenon. While anxiety can *result* from a wide variety of causes, what is different in its effect is the way in which the ego uses and experiences it. Fingarette wisely interprets this point in relation to Tillich and it is to him that I am indebted for part of the insight I feel this lends to our understanding of human anxiety. Demonstration of the linkage between Tillich's thought about anxiety and that of psychoanalysis is facilitated by a bit of "translation" undertaken by Professor Herbert Fingarette in his work *The Self in Transformation*.[11] Substituting for Tillich's metaphysical terms *non-being* and *negation*, the word *anxiety*, and reproducing Tillich's *being* and *affirmation* by *ego-functions* and *ego*, he accomplishes a remarkable bridge. Looking first at one that Fingarette finds characteristic of Tillich's more "metaphysical . . . vein," we read:

> Nonbeing is dependent on that being it negates. . . . There could be no negation if there were no preceding affirmation to be negated. . . . Secondly, non-being is dependent on the special qualities of being. In itself nonbeing has no quality

and no difference of qualities. But it gets them in relation to being. The character of the negation of being is determined by that in being which is negated. This makes it possible to speak of qualities of nonbeing and, consequently, of types of anxiety.[12]

These words and usages are unfamiliar and difficult sayings for the psychotherapist. But given Fingarette's translation (which I believe Tillich accomplishes himself in his sermons)[13] we have the following:

Anxiety is dependent on the ego-functions it negates . . . There could be no anxiety if there were no preceding ego-functioning to be negated. . . . Anxiety is dependent on the special qualities of the ego. In itself anxiety has no quality and no differences of qualities. But it gets them in relation to the ego. The character of the anxiety of the ego is determined by that in the ego which is negated. This makes it possible to speak of qualities of anxiety and, consequently, of types of anxiety.[14]

If one adds to the foregoing the corollary that one of the ego functions is object-relations, namely the attachment to persons, ideals, ideologies, and values, and that another is identification, namely the taking into oneself and making one's own certain qualities which inhere in that to which one is attached, and that anxiety results from the threat of loss by the ego of such attachment (just as grief follows the certainty of loss), then the parallel appears complete.

The ego organization is necessary to experience anxiety as such, and the quality of the ego (which entails its attachments and their character) determines the types of threats which are germane to it and the types of response to threats which will emerge when it is threatened. In other words, my capacity to be vulnerable derives from my being a person and having attachments, and the range of responses to stress that threatens these attachments and my personhood derives from the nature of my personhood and its attachments.

Tillich, in Fingarette's view and in my own, does not accept the full parallelism between the existential and pathological (or normal and neurotic) forms of anxiety. Rather, for him, "Pathological anxiety is a state of existential anxiety under special conditions."[15] And what are these special conditions? Tillich sees them from a number of points. 1) The self may seek an object for its anxiety, concretizing it, as in the case of phobia, for example. Here, however, as Odier has pointed out in *Anxiety and Magical Thinking*,[16] the ego evidences a defect through its accepting a logically unacceptable rationalization. Or, as Fingarette would put it, surrenders "to some extent the sovereignty of . . . (its) synthetic power."[17] Since the operation of the ego's synthetic function is basic to the person's perception of his own *self* as possessed of integrity, this abrogation undermines individual esteem as well as ego-functioning. 2) If anxiety is not taken up into the self through the operation of *courage* (exercise of the synthetic and integrative powers of the ego), the alternative is despair. To avoid despair the neurotic, according to Tillich, affirms a limited self, converting his existential anxiety into neurotic anxiety. "He who is not capable of a powerful self-affirmation in spite of the anxiety of non-being is forced into a weak, reduced self-affirmation."[18]

The limited self is the self each of us is doomed to be —unless and until we grow through the crisis and calm that are entailed by accepting the anxiety that Tillich calls existential and that Freud calls normal. Psychoanalysis has been preoccupied with pathology and has had too little time to study the functioning of the ego in non-pathological stages and states. Theology has been preoccupied with spiritual sickness and health but has until recently left few categories accessible to the scientist for correlation with the phenomena he observes or the theories he uses. Tillich has dealt with health as well as sickness and has seen the trials of even the well man, even as Freud knew and taught of everyday unhappiness. Neither expected a stress-free existence. Neither respected the man who sought a world free of pain or anxiety. Both acknowledged that the state of being human and civilized exacted a toll. For Freud this was seen as an inevitable clash between the instincts and culture. For Tillich it was the challenge of accepting the fact that being always implies the taking within itself of non-being and the exercise of courage *in spite of*. Both were enemies of illusions, of the truncated self, of the comforting dishonesties and illusions of religions that by-pass reality. Each sought the courage to face things as they are and the discrepancies between our wishes and our achievements. Neither could settle for an easy compromise. Both demanded a unifying and comprehensive explanatory system. For Freud this excluded religion; for Tillich it put demands upon religion which may or may not be fulfilled. As a philosopher Tillich could define these demands; as a man he could exemplify them; as a Christian he could believe that *in spite of* negation, non-being and neurosis—grace, love and courage could prevail. His optimism like Freud's pessimism was based on reality, a reality each sought and to which each sought to be true.

Notes

1. For an overview of this background, cf. Oskar Pfister, *Christianity and Fear* (New York: Macmillan, 1948), translated from the German publication in 1944; also cf. Alexander et al., *Psychoanalytic Pioneers* (New York: Basic Books, 1966).
2. Cf. *The Interpretation of History* (New York: Scribners, 1936).
3. W. G. Cole, *Sex in Christianity and Psychoanalysis* (New York: Oxford, 1955).
4. Mircea Eliade, "Paul Tillich and the History of Religions," in Paul Tillich, *The Future of Religions*, Jerald C. Brauer, ed. (New York: Harper and Row, 1966).
5. Cf. Earl A. Loomis, *The Self in Pilgrimage* (New York: Harpers, 1960).
6. *Inhibitions, Symptoms and Anxiety* (London: Hogarth, 1930), original German edition, 1926.
7. Breuer and Freud, *Studies in Hysteria* (Boston: Beacon Press, 1937), original German edition, 1895.
8. *Civilization and Its Discontents* (London: Hogarth, 1930).
9. "Totem and Taboo" in *Basic Writings* (New York: Modern Library, 1938).
10. *The Future of an Illusion* (London: Hogarth, 1927).
11. Herbert Fingarette, *The Self in Transformation* (New York: Basic Books, 1953).
12. *Ibid.*, p. 92. The Quote is from Paul Tillich, *The Courage to Be* (New Haven: Yale University Press, 1959), p. 40.

13. Contrast his simplicity when speaking as a preacher with ponderous discoursing as a metaphysician.
14. Fingarette, op. cit., p. 93.
15. Tillich, op. cit., p. 65
16. Charles Odier, *Anxiety and Magical Thinking* (New York: International Universities Press, 1956).
17. Fingarette, op cit., p. 94.
18. Tillich, op. cit., p. 66.

Appendix

Paul Tillich's Letter
of 23 May 1943 to Thomas Mann*

On 12 April 1943, during his preparation for the writing of *Dr. Faustus*, Thomas Mann requested of Professor Paul Tillich as accurate a description as possible of the course of study of a German theologian around the year 1900. He required details, authentic details, to enable him to "realize" Adrian Leverkühn's study of theology. Mann's letter of request seems no longer to be extant, though Mann fortunately did preserve Professor Tillich's reply of 23 May 1943 among his *Dr. Faustus* papers. We reproduce this letter with the friendly approval and consent of the late Professor Tillich. Thomas Mann's underlinings, which are italicized in the German original, are omitted from this translation. The footnotes were added by the German editor.

Union Theological Seminary
Broadway at 120th Street
New York

May 23, 1943

Mr. Thomas Mann
1550 San Remo Drive
Pacific Palisades, California

Dear Mr. Thomas Mann:

Sincere thanks for your letter. Having finished my "term papers" yesterday, I have commenced my answer today. Though

* Originally published in "Aus den Materialien zum Dr. Faustus," *Blatter der Thomas-Mann-Gesellschaft*, 5 (1965). Reproduced here for the first time in English by the kind permission of Katja (Mrs. Thomas) Mann and the Thomas-Mann-Gesellschaft in Zurich, Switzerland. (H. A. B., translator).

it might be personally more satisfying to respond to your questions by means of a biographical essay, I believe you will be better served by a "piecemeal" answer to your questions. Besides, this kind of response requires less time.

The program of theological studies at German universities at the century's turn commenced after graduation from a humanistic gymnasium. Prerequisites were a knowledge of Greek and Latin and in most cases also of Hebrew.

I myself registered in the theological program in Berlin in the fall of 1904. In the spring of 1905 I went to Tübingen and in the fall of 1905 to Halle where I studied for four semesters. In the fall of 1907 I returned to Berlin and took my first theological examination before the consistory of Brandenburg in the winter of 1909, and my second theological examination before the same body in 1912. I was ordained by the General Superintendent of Brandenburg in August of 1912. In the meantime I had taken my Ph.D. in Breslau in 1910 and my licentiate of theology in Halle in 1911. I tell you all this only because it represents a typical program for an evangelical theologian preparing himself for practical service and also for an academic career.

Minimally, the course of study was no less than three years, though it usually was extended to four. Following completion of the course, preparation lasting a year or more commenced for the first theological examination. About one-half year of this period was devoted to the major writing requirements. Theological study was so organized as to devote the first years to exegetical and historical subjects, the middle years to systematic theology, and the concluding years to applied subjects such as homiletics, religious education, personal ministry, etc. The curriculum was flexible, however, and allowed students to vary the order of their study so as to suit their predilections for certain subjects or professors. Lectures and seminars characterized theological study just as any other. The seminars of Harnack and Troeltsch and Holl had a worldwide influence whose effects I still discern daily here in the USA. As a university lecturer (*Privatdozent*) in theology I myself introduced the discussion period into the lectures, a practice which was not yet common in my time. The study of philosophy received a varying emphasis depending on the faculty, though philosophy remained a regular mandatory part of the first theological examination. The second theological examination, which followed the first or second year of applied studies, naturally emphasized practical applications. Philosophy got its major emphasis in Württemberg where the Tübingen Foundation (*Tübinger Stift*) in the best old tradition commenced with two years of philosophical study. The normal combination of subjects in which we had to stand examination were, in addition to philosophy, Old Testament; New Testament (an exegetical understanding of the original text, the historical introduction thereto, and the historical development of theological concepts of both testaments); ancient, medieval and modern church history (which obviously included much secular historical material); systematic theology (including history of dogma); ethics (philosophical and theological); applied or practical theology in the various areas of ecclesiastical activity. The field of music received attention in liturgical history, indeed, in a very substantial way.

When I began my studies the (Halle) theological faculty was second only to that of Berlin, much superior to the one at Leipzig, which suffered from doctrinal restrictions, and in active competition with the liberal one at Marburg. Two traditions rubbed elbows in Halle, the pietistic deriving from August Hermann Francke and his orphan's homes in Halle, and the rationalistic stemming from the Wolffian period and the Enlightenment. Theology at Halle in my day was a mixture of conservative traditional theology and Ritchlianism. The dominating personality of the first type was Martin Kaehler,[1] who in his youth was an inspired student of classical literature and philosophy, boasting with relevance to the rest of us that he once knew all of Goethe's prime works from memory. Subsequently, however, he fell victim to the revivalist movement of the middle of the last century and contraposed the Pauline gospel of sin and redemption to the aesthetic humanism of the great "pagan" Goethe, as he was wont to call him. All others seemed minor to us when compared to the stature of this man Kaehler. We attended his lectures not because of the systematic theology he taught rather drily and from a textbook but for the sake of what as students we referred to as "fringe benefits," namely, his interpolations which influenced all of us profoundly throughout our maturity. My friends and I owe to him the realization that our thinking also is broken and requires "justification," and that dogmatism is consequently the intellectual analog of phariseeism.

The strongest proponents of so-called liberal theology were in Berlin and Marburg. Wilhelm Hermann in Marburg was the counterpart of Martin Kaehler in Halle. Much more so than Harnack and Troeltsch, Hermann was a person of great ethical and religious force and even today is venerated by people such as my President Coffin of Union Theological Seminary, a student of his, in the same way I revere Martin Kaehler.

The difference between the two theological views was viable in two areas. Liberal theology, represented by such scholars as Ritschl, Harnack and Troeltsch, had adopted the historical critical method of secular historiography, whereas the traditional conservatives held tenaciously to the idea of revelation and sought to defend traditional exegesis. I myself and many of my friends adhered to liberal theology, on the one hand, for its scholarly superiority was unquestionable. Contrariwise, however, we found it impossible to agree with the theological position of the liberals. It seemed to us that they lacked insight into the "daemonic" character of human existence (in the same sense that I propagated my theology which had evolved between the Great Wars and which established itself on a broad basis, in part through the assistance of Reinhold Niebuhr, as opposed to the prevailing liberal moralism and humanism.) We concluded that the conservative tradition had preserved more of the true understanding of human nature and of the tragedy of existence than had the liberal progressive bourgeois ideology. Already at that time Kierkegaard was exercising a strong influence on a small group of theological students at Halle. In our view liberal theology lacked profundity and paradox and I am convinced that world history has proved our view correct.

These observations serve to answer your question about the anti-metaphysical-ethical-epistemological character of Ritschlian theology. All of that derives in fact from Kant, but only in the sense of the completely one-sided so-called neo-Kantian interpretation, which must be regarded as resulting from the great shock-experience of the Forties of the preceding century. I mean the shock accruing from the collapse of Hegel's effort at the ontological[2] synthesis of Christianity and philosophy. Ritschlian theology is a typical escape-theology. It attempts to find a firm bulwark against universally triumphant naturalism in the ethical personality but does not venture to attack this naturalism. Naturalism is regarded as given but is supposed to lack any power in *one* (underlined by Tillich) area, namely, in the sphere of values. (The subsequent Ritschlian School developed in close association with value-philosophy.) The surrender by this means to the mechanism of the bourgeois worldview of all reality, nature, and history, was scarcely noticed because of the joy of having found an apparently secure island. Marx, Nietzsche, Freud, et al. prove that this security was only an apparent one. As a theological student at Halle I demanded in opposition to this view "the theology of attack" in place of defense. This obviously means metaphysics, above all the interpretation of history. The followers of Ritschl appealed with only a partial right to the Reformers. Though neither Luther nor Calvin, the destroyers of scholastic metaphysics, provide an explicit metaphysic, both of them reveal an implicit metaphysic in their doctrine of God. The entire intellectual-spiritual history of Germany, including Boehme, Schelling, Nietzsche, cannot be understood apart from Luther's stance toward nature. This view includes, of course, a specific form of mysticism, which was attacked by Ritschl and his followers in an almost fanatic manner. The consequence was the cold moralism that characterizes this entire theology with the single exception of Hermann.

In response to your question regarding the cultural affirmation of liberal theology, I can say only that it did indeed represent a far-reaching adaptation to the ideals of bourgeois society, above all by emphasizing as strongly as possible the ethically based personality ideal. Religiosity became, so to speak, a function of humanness, measured by the yardstick of the developing ethical personality. The ecstatic and paradoxical aspects of the religious were reduced to an ethical faith in progress. I would venture to assert that theologians of the type of Kaehler and Dorner and our group, who sought at that time to renew classical German philosophy, were much more passionately devoted to culture than was the naively conventional Ritschlian bourgeois view.

So-called dialectical theology is entirely a product of the postwar period and has no relation to the development of students prior to the First War. Kierkegaard did not become effective till between the Great Wars, either in theology or in philosophy. One could perhaps regard the so-called dialectical (actually paradoxical and subsequently supra-naturalistic) theology of Barth as the expression of the catastrophe-experience following the First War of those who had grown up in the liberal tradition. Barth's effect on the students in the middle of the twenties was extraordinary. One can assert that real liberalism was dead or transmuted in the German universities of the mid-twenties. The liberal remnants were all too easily inclined to move over into the camp of the German Christians. (One could already observe during the First War that liberal theologians were becoming nationalistic and thereby eligible for membership on church boards.)

It might be of interest for your project to know that I belonged to the Christian Student Organization called "Wingolf" and that the summer of 1907, when I was the "First Officer" of this seventy-man group, seems to me even today yet to have been the greatest chapter of my life. Whatever I have become in a theological, philosophical, and human sense I owe only in part to the professors but contrariwise in an overwhelming measure to that organization whose theological and philosophical debates after midnight and the ensuing personal conversations before sunrise became decisive for my entire life. Music played a large part in all this. And the romantic relationship to nature, which in all my current class lectures I place in deliberate contrast to the Calvinistic-American estrangement from nature, I owe in the first instance to my trip at that time through Thuringia and to the Wartburg in the company of my fraternals.

Your inquiry about a massive orthodoxy with diabolical miracles, belief in heaven and hell in a mythological sense, is not easy to answer. The orthodox Lutheran theology of that day as it obtained in Leipzig, Erlangen, Greifswald unquestionably sought to preserve as much as possible all the elements of biblical religion. And yet faith in the devil played no part at that time, one simply did not bother about it even while pleading for some kind of personally conceived satanic principle. I never encountered any disposition to relate events or objects, for example, injurious animals and the like, to the devil, and conservative theologians would have rejected any such disposition as a denial of the doctrine of creation. By contrast, the faith in miracles, the question of the credibility of historical criticism, the Christological problem were prominent. The opposition between the positive (orthodox) and liberal theologians was sharp in this respect. Both, however, interpreted expressions such as heaven and hell symbolically (identifying hell with god-absence and heaven with god-presence). Extremely important was the question of the physical resurrection of Jesus inasmuch as dogmatic, historical-critical, and piety motives were combined in this question. The triumph of the historical-critical school was decisive for the liberal interpretation of all questions involving historical problems. By the mid-twenties such problems as the physical resurrection of Jesus had become inconsequential, and even persons such as Barth explained unequivocally that they acquiesced in the historical judgments of scientific criticism. My colleague Bultmann in Marburg combined the greatest radicalism in historical criticism (surpassing Harnack and Troeltsch by far) with a passionate acceptance of Barthian theology. In all these matters the tremendousness of the upheaval resulting from the First Great War cannot be over-emphasized. From a purely factual point of view, the passing shortly before, during, and immediately after the First War of a whole generation of theologians who dominated the period 1890–1914 was also reflected in the great upheaval.

I think that I may perhaps have provided adequate answers to most of your questions. If not, I shall be most happy to respond to any others you have.

I look forward with great anticipation to the chapter into which you incorporate these materials.

With sincere greetings, I remain yours.

/s/ Paul Tillich
Professor Paul Tillich.

Notes

1. Ehrenfried Kumpf in *Dr. Faustus* (New York, 1948, p. 95) was originally also intended to bear Luther's Christian name.
2. Thomas Mann wrote in with pencil above this *seinsmassig* ("being-related") and below it, "ontological proof for the existence of God derived from the concept of God."

The Contributors

Dr. John Herman Randall, Jr.

One of America's most distinguished philosophers, Dr. *JOHN HERMAN RANDALL, JR.* has spent his entire teaching career at Columbia University where since 1951 he has been F. J. E. Woodbridge Professor of Philosophy. A graduate of Columbia (B.A., 1918; M.A., 1919; Ph.D., 1922) he also holds an honorary Litt.D., from Ohio Wesleyan University. Dr. Randall is a Fellow of the American Academy of Arts and Sciences, a past president of the Renaissance Society of America and a member of the American Philosophical Association.

A close associate of Dr. Tillich's during his teaching career at Union Theological Seminary, Dr. Randall is the author of *Philosophy of Paul Tillich*, published in 1952. A prolific writer, Dr. Randall has authored some twenty-eight books in the fields of philosophy and religion, including *The Making of the Modern Mind; The Role of Knowledge in Western Religion; Nature and Historical Experience; Studies in the History of Ideas; Freedom and Experience;* and *The Philosophy of Ernst Cassirer.* He is also honorary editor of the *Journal of Philosophy.*

Dr. Roger Lincoln Shinn

Widely acclaimed in theological circles as an eminent scholar and perceptive social critic, Dr. Roger Lincoln Shinn, as William E. Dodge, Jr. Professor of Applied Christianity, holds one of the most distinguished theological chairs in American Protestantism, succeeding in this post the dean of American theologians, Reinhold Niebuhr. A native of Ohio, Dr. Shinn graduated from Heidelberg College (B.A., 1938); Union Theological Seminary (B.D., 1941)

113

and Columbia University (Ph.D., 1951). He has been the recipient of three honorary degrees, awarded by Mission House Theological Seminary (D.D., 1960), Heidelberg College (Litt.D., 1963) and Franklin Marshall College (D.D., 1963).

Dr. Shinn has served successively as chairman of the Philosophy Department at Heidelberg College (1949–54), Professor of Theology (1954–57), and Professor of Christian Ethics (1957–59) at the Divinity School of Vanderbilt University. Prior to his present appointment, he served as Professor of Christian Ethics at Union Theological Seminary. He has been Earl Lecturer at the Pacific School of Religion in 1957, William Belden Noble Lecturer at Harvard University in 1960 and Cole Lecturer at Vanderbilt in 1965.

Dr. Shinn's publications include: *Beyond This Darkness; Christianity and the Problem of History; Life, Death and Destiny; The Existentialist Posture; The Sermon on The Mount;* and *The Search for Identity:* Essays on the American Character (Editor). He has also contributed chapters and essays to a number of books, including *Christian Faith and Social Action, Weltkirchen Lexicon, Nuclear Weapons* and *The Conflict of Conscience and Christian Faith* and *The Contemporary Arts.*

A colleague of Dr. Tillich, Professor Shinn has also been active in numerous church, community and learned organizations. He is a member of the American Theological Society, Americans for Democratic Action, the General Committee of the Departments of Racial and Cultural Relations, and the Department of Church and Economic Life of the National Council of Churches, the Religious Advisory Council to the President's Committee on Government Contracts and the Committee for Racial Justice Now of the United Church of Christ.

He is president of the board for Homeland Ministries of the United Church of Christ and served in 1957 as consultant to the North American Conference on Faith and Order of the World Council of Churches.

Dr. Earl Alfred Loomis, Jr.

A pioneer in the field of religion and psychiatry, DR. EARL ALFRED LOOMIS, JR., is a practicing psychiatrist in New York

City. Born in Minneapolis, Dr. Loomis holds degrees from the University of Minnesota (B.A., 1942; B.S., 1943; B.M., 1945; M.D., 1946). He served as Instructor in Psychiatry and a Fellow in Internal Medicine at the University of Pennsylvania (1949–52), Associate Professor of Child Psychiatry at the University of Pittsburgh (1952–56), and Chief of the Division of Child Psychiatry and Associate Attending Psychiatrist at St. Luke's Hospital in New York from 1956–59.

While at St. Luke's, Dr. Loomis also accepted the appointment as Professor of Psychiatry and Religion and first Director of the Program in Psychiatry and Religion at Union Theological Seminary. The primary goal of this program is to explore and further the interrelations of psychiatry and theology at every level of training of theological students. The program also encourages continuous interchange of thought between the disciplines of psychiatry and theology.

Dr. Loomis has also lectured at Western Theological Seminary, Philadelphia Divinity School and Pittsburgh-Xenia Theological Seminary. He is a member of the American Medical Association, and a fellow of the Orthopsychiatric Association, the Psychoanalytic Association, the Academy of Child Psychiatry, and the College of Physicians. He wrote *The Self in Pilgrimage* published in New York by Harper, 1960.

The manuscript was edited by Ralph R. Busick. The book was designed by Barbara Engel. The type face for the book is Linotype Palatino designed by Hermann Zapf in 1950; and the display face is also Palatino.

The book was printed on S. D. Warren's Olde Style Antique paper and bound in Columbia Mills' Bayside Vellum over boards. Manufactured in the United States of America.